Bobby Owsinski's
DECONSTRUCTED HITS
CLASSIC ROCK Vol. 1

Bobby Owsinski's
DECONSTRUCTED HITS

CLASSIC ROCK Vol. 1

Uncover the stories & techniques behind 20 iconic songs

Alfred Music
LEARN · TEACH · PLAY

LOS ANGELES

Alfred Music
P.O. Box 10003
Van Nuys, CA 91410-0003
alfred.com

Produced in association with Lawson Music Media, Inc.
Library of Congress Control Number: 2013950890

ISBN-10: 0-7390-9389-4
ISBN-13: 978-0-7390-9389-4

Cover illustration: record: © Dreamstime.com / Aureiko

 **Alfred Cares.** Contents printed on 100% recycled paper.

CONTENTS

Preface VII

How to Listen...VIII

Advanced Listening Technique..IX

Characteristics of the Average Hit Song..XI

The Five Elements of a Great Arrangement XII

The Hit Song Secret XIII

THE HITS

The Jimi Hendrix Experience
All Along the Watchtower 3

Cream
Sunshine of Your Love.. 9

The Rolling Stones
Gimme Shelter 15

Frank Zappa
Peaches en Regalia 21

Led Zeppelin
Stairway to Heaven.... 27

Rod Stewart
Maggie May.. 33

The Who
Won't Get Fooled Again 39

Joe Walsh and Barnstorm
Rocky Mountain Way 45

Aerosmith
Dream On... 51

Stevie Wonder
Living for the City 57

Bruce Springsteen
Born to Run 63

Boston
  More than a Feeling.. 69

KISS
  Detroit Rock City 75

David Bowie
  Suffragette City 81

The Eagles
  Hotel California 87

Dire Straits
  Sultans of Swing.. 95

Tom Petty and the Heartbreakers
  Refugee.. 101

Rush
  Tom Sawyer 107

AC/DC
  Back in Black 113

Phil Collins
  In the Air Tonight.. 119

Glossary.. 125

Bobby Owsinski Bibliography.. 131

PREFACE

Of all the regular posts on my Big Picture music production blog (bobbyowsinski.blogspot.com), the most popular are always the ones involving the analysis of hit songs.

I first started doing these analyses after finding a few isolated tracks from various hits (which almost everyone loves to hear) on YouTube and providing some commentary on them. Slowly that turned into a much deeper analysis, similar to those I've included in a couple of my books to illustrate how an arrangement in a hit song actually works. Eventually I expanded on that idea to encompass a lot more than the arrangement, and that's what you'll read here. Now, each song analysis looks at the song itself (its form and lyrics), the arrangement, the sound, and its production, as well as some key song facts and trivia.

While you're reading these analyses, try listening to each song, and I guarantee you'll begin to hear it differently than ever before. You'll find yourself listening *through* the song instead of to it. Rather than the wash of a complete mix, you'll begin to hear all of the individual parts of the arrangement, the production tricks, and the audio intricacies. Most of all, my aim is to identify and highlight the tangible reasons for why the song was not only a hit, but also an enduring one. Every hit has an intangible factor to it that can't be described, but there's a lot under the hood that absolutely can.

I hope you'll enjoy reading these song analyses as much as I did making them. They are a great learning tool for any engineer, producer, songwriter, or musician, as they really do help you to look deep inside the actual workings of a hit. If you're just a fan, you'll enjoy them too, because you'll listen to some of your favorite songs in a completely new and different way.

How to Listen

Since you're reading a book about listening to music (actually *through* the music), it's helpful to have a few pointers on what to listen for. Here I break it down to a general listening technique and then add an additional advanced listening technique for musicians and engineers, who probably already have more refined listening skills. If you aren't familiar with a term, check out its meaning in the glossary at the end of the book.

General Listening Technique

While this might seem like a long list, these are just some of the things that an experienced studio ear will hear almost automatically. You can train yourself to do the same pretty easily. Just start with a few at a time, and before you know it, you'll naturally be listening *through* the song, instead of just hearing it. Beware that after listening like this, you can sometimes get too analytical and lose the enjoyment of the song for a while (it happens to most first-year college music and audio students).

- **Listen for the instruments that are providing the pulse to the song.** All music, even dreamlike ambient music, has a pulse, and that's the first thing you want to notice.

- **Listen to the ambience.** Does a vocal or an instrument sound like it's in the room right in front of you, or in a club, a church, or a cave? Is there an audible reverb tail? Can you hear it repeat after it stops playing?

- **Listen to the clarity of the mix.** Can you hear each instrument and vocal clearly in the mix? Are some buried so you can't distinguish what they are? Can you identify all the instruments that you're hearing?

- **Listen to the clarity of each instrument or vocal.** Does it sound lifelike or distorted? Is there an effect used to alter its sound?

- **Try to identify each section of the song.** Is something new happening the second and third time you hear a section? Is there a new vocal or instrument introduced? Is one taken away? Is an effect added or subtracted?

- **Try to identify the loudest thing in the mix.** Is the vocal louder than the other instruments or is it lower than the rest of the band? Is the bass out in front of the drums?

- **Identify the hook of the song.** What instrument or vocal plays it? When does it occur? Is it built around a lyric? Does it even have one?

- **Listen to the stereo soundfield of the song.** Are there instruments or vocals that only appear on one side? Are there instruments that appear on both sides?

- **Listen to the overall timbre of the song.** Does it seem bright? Too much bass? Is there an instrument or vocal that stands out because of its timbre?

- **Listen to the dynamics of the song.** Does it breath volume-wise with the song's pulse? Does it sound lifeless or do the instruments and vocals sound natural like you'd hear in a club?

- **Is the song fun to listen to?** Why? Why not?

ADVANCED LISTENING TECHNIQUE

The following guidelines are for those readers who have some musical or studio knowledge, who may want to listen with a bit more precision.

- **Listen for the time signature.** Where's the downbeat and how many beats until the next one?

- **Listen for the number of different sections in the song.** Do the sections repeat? Does the song have a bridge? Is there an interlude between sections?

- **Listen for the number of bars in each section.** How long is each section? Is it the same length the next time it repeats? Are there any extra bars of music? All music isn't symmetrical in that it won't necessarily have 4-, 8-, 12-, or 16-bar sections, and in many cases you'll find an extra bar before or after a section.

- **Listen to the chord pattern(s) of the song.** Does it change from the verse to the chorus or bridge? Does it change the next time the section repeats? Is there a key change in the song?

- **Listen to the song's melody.** Are there big jumps, and if so, in what section are they?

- **Listen for any delays on individual instruments.** Is the delay timed to the track so the repeats are in sync with the pulse of the song? Is the same delay used on multiple instruments or are there different ones?

- **Listen to the ambience of the song.** Is there more than one environment? Does each one have the same decay? Does each one have the same timbre?

- **Listen for the compression in the song.** Can you identify which instruments are compressed? Can you hear the compressor working? Does the song sound more or less compressed than other songs you're familiar with?

- **Are there any doubled instruments or vocals?** Are they panned in stereo?

There are a number of other listening details besides these, but these are good starting points. Of course, the song analysis will point most of them out with more precision as you read and listen along. Happy listening!

CHARACTERISTICS OF THE AVERAGE HIT SONG

Here are some interesting characteristics common to hit songs including those in this book. You won't find them all in every song, but the majority of hit songs exhibit at least some of these traits.

- **Most hit songs have a short intro.** It's always been about getting to the point, and that never seems to change.

- **The melody in the chorus tends to be higher in pitch than the verses.** This builds intensity and energy as the song progresses.

- **The chorus and the bridge have more intensity than the verse.** This is due to either more instruments or vocals entering, or greater performance intensity from the players.

- **The song's intensity builds from beginning to end.** Most songs start off less intense, and then gradually grow with each section. It then peaks towards the end of the song, either on the bridge or the outro choruses.

- **The ending can date a song.** Songs before 2000 tended to use fade endings, but more recent songs tend to use a hard ending. Hard endings are said to play better in the digital world, where a fade is more likely to make the listener skip on to the next song.

As you go through the songs in the book you'll see a number of similarities in song form, arrangement, and production. That will be a great help if you're a songwriter, arranger, or producer. The more you know about how hits are made, the more likely you'll actually have one.

Keep in mind that even though you may not like a song or an artist, it's still worth checking out the song analysis. Hits are hits for a reason, and they are definitely hard to come by. Every song included here has some sort of magic as well as some common elements, so something can be learned from every single one.

THE FIVE ELEMENTS OF A GREAT ARRANGEMENT

Before we look at the first song, here's an overview of the five elements of a great arrangement, which is something you'll see in every song analysis.

Most well-conceived arrangements are limited in the number of arrangement elements that occur at the same time. An element can be a single instrument such as a lead guitar or a vocal, or it can be a group of instruments such as the bass and drums, a doubled guitar line, a group of backing vocals, and so on. Generally, a group of instruments playing exactly the same rhythm is considered an element. Examples include a doubled lead guitar or doubled vocal, both single elements even though there are two of them; also a lead vocal with two additional harmonies. Two lead guitars playing different parts can be two elements, however. A lead and a rhythm guitar can be two separate elements as well.

The five main arrangement elements are:

- **The Foundation (the rhythm section):** The foundation is usually the bass and drums, but can also include a rhythm guitar and/or keyboards if they're playing the same rhythmic figure as the rhythm section. Occasionally, as in the case of power trios, the foundation element will only consist of drums since the bass will usually have to play a different rhythm figure to fill out the sound, so it becomes its own element.

- **The Pad:** A pad is a long sustaining note or chord. In the days before synthesizers, a Hammond Organ provided the best pad and was joined later by the Fender Rhodes. Synthesizers now provide the majority of pads but real strings or a guitar power chord can also suffice.

- **The Rhythm:** Rhythm is any instrument that plays counter to the foundation element. This can be a double-time shaker or tambourine, a rhythm guitar strumming on the backbeat, or congas playing a Latin feel. The rhythm element is used to add motion and excitement to the track.

- **The Lead:** A lead vocal, lead instrument, or solo.

- **The Fills:** Fills generally occur in the spaces between lead lines, or they can be signature hook lines. You can think of a fill element as an answer to the lead.

Most arrangements have these five elements, but very rarely are they all present at the same time. Sometimes as few as three occur simultaneously, but any more than five elements at the same time is confusing to the listener, and usually causes listener fatigue as a result.

Take note that none of the hit songs in this book have more than five elements happening at once, which is your first lesson in creating a hit.

THE HIT SONG SECRET

A movie director once told me, "If you can get the viewer to laugh just once and cry just once in a movie, you'll have a hit." It seems like there's an analogy to that in the record business as well, as indicated 20 years ago by British psychologist John Sloboda and verified in 2007 by John Guhn of the University of British Columbia.

Sloboda conducted an experiment in which he asked listeners to identify passages in a song that register a strong emotion such as tears or goose bumps. The listeners found 20 such passages which Sloboda then analyzed; he found that 18 contained a writing device known as *appoggiatura*. An appoggiatura can be a passing note that clashes with the melody just enough to create a temporary dissonance, an entrance of a new voice, or song dynamics, all of which create tension for the listener.

All art is based around tension and release. In painting, it's black against white. In photography, it's light against the shadows. In music, it's dissonance against harmony or quiet against loud. Tension and release makes things interesting. You can't have any kind of art without it.

When several appoggiaturas happen close to one another in a melody, it develops a constant state of tension and release, which makes the melody of a song more powerful and provokes an even stronger reaction from the listener.

It turns out that there is actually a formula for appoggiatura that's comprised of four elements:

- Passages that go from quiet to loud
- An entrance of a new instrument or harmony
- A melody that suddenly expands its range
- Unexpected deviations of melody or harmony

All of these are great songwriting and arrangement devices that I'll point out in the upcoming song analyses. The fact that there have been actual studies that verify what we intuitively know shows that there may be some validity to the fact that there's a sort of formula to making hits, even though it's usually not something the songwriter consciously thinks about. One thing's for sure: surprises in volume level, melody, and harmony are what makes a listener's spine tingle. The next time you listen to a song, be on the lookout for one.

The Jimi Hendrix Experience

All Along the Watchtower

SONG FACTS

Album: *Electric Ladyland*
Writer: Bob Dylan
Producer: Jimi Hendrix
Studios: Olympic Studios (London), Record Plant (New York City)
Release Date: September 21, 1968
Length: 4:00
Sales: 2+ million (album)
Highest Chart Position: #20 U.S. Billboard Hot 100, #5 U.K. Singles Chart

What is almost certainly the definitive Jimi Hendrix song is one he didn't write himself. "All Along the Watchtower" was written by Bob Dylan and released in 1967 on Dylan's *John Wesley Harding* album. The album was given to Hendrix by a publicist who worked for Dylan's manager Albert Grossman.

Recording of Hendrix's version of the song began at Olympic Studios in London on a 4-track tape recorder with Experience members Mitch Mitchell on drums and Noel Redding on bass, along with Traffic guitarist Dave Mason on 12-string guitar. On take 7, Redding, dissatisfied with how long the process was taking, left for the pub and Mason took over on bass. On takes 11 and 12, Stones guitarist Brain Jones arrived at the studio intoxicated and insisted on playing piano. After playing poorly, he was asked to leave and Mason returned to 12-string as they recorded the next takes without a bass player.

Take 27 eventually became the keeper, after which, Hendrix himself added the bass. All subsequent overdubs and mixing took place at the Record Plant in New York City, first on a 12-track tape deck, then, eventually, on a 16-track. Even after a first version of the mix was completed, Hendrix was dissatisfied and continued to add instruments for a number of months afterwards. Despite having the additional tracks of the 16-track deck to play with, many parts had to be erased to make room for his new ideas.

Rolling Stone magazine has named "All Along the Watchtower" #47 of its *500 Greatest Songs of All Time*, while Britain's *Total Guitar* has it as the #1 greatest cover song of all time. Even though Bob Dylan wrote the song, he still considers the Hendrix interpretation to be the definitive version; according to Dylan's own notes accompanying his *Biograph* album, to this day, when he plays the song live, it is closer to that version as a tribute.

THE SONG

"All Along the Watchtower" is made up of a single set of chord changes that repeats over and over. There are no other sections besides the three verses; the solos occur over those same verse chord changes. On that alone you would think this would be a boring song, but that's not the case thanks to a constantly changing palette of sounds. The form looks like this:

intro 1 | intro 2 | verse | solo | verse | solo | solo | solo | verse | outro

The lyrics are more like poetry put to music than anything, which, of course, is the strength of Bob Dylan. The hook "All Along the Watchtower" is stated only once at the beginning of the last verse, yet it's such a strong image that it supersedes the other lyrics by far.

THE ARRANGEMENT

"All Along the Watchtower" begins with the bass, drums, and the acoustic 12-string playing the intro, which is punctuated with a vibraslap on beat 4 of every bar. There is a little twist which makes it totally interesting, but uncountable if you're tapping along, where a half-beat guitar pick-up goes into the instrumental intro with the famous lead guitar solo line. At this point, the rest of the band enters with more intensity.

On the first verse you can feel the band pull back dynamically as the music gets less intense to make room for the vocal. A new, dark-sounding, strumming electric guitar enters on the left that acts like glue for the track, and the tambourine adds the high frequencies as it pushes it along. At the end of bar 16 (halfway through the verse), the bass and rhythm guitar play the next to last chord as a IV chord, while the 12-string guitar plays it as a VI, and this occurs during the last two vocal verses as well. Throughout the verse, a lead guitar plays fills after each vocal phrase.

During the first solo, the intensity once again builds with the drums and tambourine switching again to double time, then the intensity lowers slightly for the second verse but still staying with the double-time feel. Once again, the lead guitar fills in the holes between the vocal phrases.

In the solo section, the first solo is similar to the previous lead sections in intensity and clean tone of the lead guitar, but the second solo changes to the verse feel. Here, the bass also changes from a loose, ad-libbed part to one that's structured on fifths, while the slide lead guitar pans from side to side. The next solo keeps the same feel but the lead guitar changes to a wah, which again pans left to right. The last part of the solo increases in intensity while the guitar changes back to a slightly overdriven Strat sound.

The last verse is identical in structure to the previous two. The outro solo section differs in that the 12-string guitar is replaced with a 6-string acoustic, strumming a more aggressive double-time pattern, while the guitar and vocal ad-libs pan back and forth over the ending fade.

Arrangement Elements

The Foundation: Bass and drums
The Rhythm: 12-string acoustic guitar, 6-string acoustic at the end, tambourine
The Pad: Strummed low-register electric guitar low in the mix
The Lead: Lead vocal, lead guitars
The Fills: Lead guitar

THE SOUND

"All Along the Watchtower" provides an interesting glimpse into the old recording world of 4-track as well as the then-new world of multitrack, all within the same song. You can hear the old world primarily on the drums and percussion, which were mixed in mono onto a single track. To make them sound stereo, they're panned hard to the left and slightly delayed to hard right, which sounds somewhat odd as there's a big hole in the middle as a result. This actually works to the song's advantage as the center is filled up nicely with the different guitars and the vocal. The tambourine, which subtly plays a big part in the song, gets the same stereo treatment as the drums. The bass is panned slightly to the left and the 12-string is panned slightly to the right.

Where the new multitrack world enters is around all of the different guitar layers in the song. Virtually every solo has a different guitar sound, and there's a very low and dark, but important, strummed electric guitar on the left that works as the glue for the song. On the outro the 12-string turns into 6-string acoustic.

There are a lot of effects layers in the song made up of several delays and delayed reverb. Except for the delay used to double them, the drums and tambourine are dry, but all of the other guitars have a slight delayed reverb which blends the track together well. The vocals and many of the guitars receive what sounds to be about a 350-millisecond tape delay which repeats about four times. Since it's tape, the frequency response is limited to begin with (most tape used for tape delay wears out during the session due to oxide wearing off, and the high frequencies suffer as a result), so the delays decay seamlessly into the track

🔊))) **Listen Up**

To the vibraslap on beat 4 of each measure of the intro.

To the long reverb tail on the 12-string guitar in the intro before the vibraslap enters.

To the solos in the middle of song that pan left to right and back again, but the echo remains on the right.

To how the 12-string acoustic guitar on the right channel turns into a 6-string acoustic strumming a different pattern on the outro.

THE PRODUCTION

"All Along the Watchtower" began as a co-production between Hendrix and his manager Chas Chandler (who produced his previous two albums), but Chandler quit early in the process over Hendrix's irregular studio habits and the fact that it was taking so long to accomplish anything. Without hearing the previous takes of the song, it's difficult to say if a better one was played before the keeper at 27, but you have to like Hendrix's instincts on keeping the one he did, as well as the many guitar overdubs it took to complete the song. The process was the total opposite of the quick recording of his previous records. The song has stood the test of time and, considering its simple form, a big reason for that can be attributed to its production.

Cream

Sunshine of Your Love

SONG FACTS

Album: *Disraeli Gears*
Writers: Jack Bruce, Pete Brown, Eric Clapton
Producer: Felix Pappalardi
Studio: Atlantic Studios (New York City)
Release Date: January 1968
Length: 4:10 (album version), 3:03 (single edit)
Sales: 500,000+ (single), 1+ million (album)
Highest Chart Position: #5 U.S. Billboard Hot 100, #25 U.K. Singles Chart

Here's a classic song that's been a big influence on generations of guitar players. "Sunshine of Your Love," by Cream, was the first single from the band's second album, *Disraeli Gears*, which was released in 1967. The song broke the band in the United States, eventually rising to #5 on the U.S. Billboard Hot 100. It was their first single to chart higher in the U.S. than in the United Kingdom.

In typical record-label fashion, Atlantic CEO Ahmet Ertegun hated both Jack Bruce (he didn't think the bass player should be the lead singer of the band) and the song, so it was almost left off the album. Although the execs at Atlantic didn't think much of the song, Bruce was always confident in its potential success, mostly because of the support he received from two of the biggest stars of the legendary Stax Records label (which Atlantic distributed at the time). Both Otis Redding and Booker T. Jones of Booker T. & the MG's loved the song and actively lobbied for its inclusion on the album. Still, it was only added because

9

of a last-minute decision when they didn't have enough material. Leave it to a record exec to want to nix what would become their biggest hit!

Rolling Stone magazine went on to name it the 65th greatest song of all time, while VH1 called it the 44th best hard rock song of all time. To almost every guitar player, it's an icon.

THE SONG

"Sunshine of Your Love" is basically a 12-bar blues song, but it's quite unusual in that it's in $\frac{8}{8}$ time rather than the usual $\frac{4}{4}$. The distinctive bass riff is 8 beats long, and the rest of the song is built around it. As with most 12-bar blues songs, the first 8 bars (sometimes 10) make up the verse and the last 4 (or 2 in some songs) make up what basically amounts to a chorus, although we generally call the full 12 bars just a verse. The song form looks like this:

intro (4 bars) | verse | interlude (2 bars) | verse |
solo (over a verse) | verse | 2 bar chorus repeat | outro

According to bassist Jack Bruce, the signature bass riff was inspired by Jimi Hendrix. The lyrics were written by beat poet Pete Brown during an all-night writing session. In an interview, Bruce said he picked up his double bass and played the riff. Pete looked out the window and the sun was coming up. Guitarist Eric Clapton later wrote the chorus.

Unlike most song lyrics, Brown was a real poet and you can tell, as the words have an elegance that's missing in the majority of hit songs that you hear today. The melody is also unusual for a blues song in that it varies from section to section.

THE ARRANGEMENT

This is early rock at its finest in that the song is just the band playing with a single overdub, and that's the guitar solo. Everything else is the simple three-piece power trio that Cream was. The only thing slightly unique is that they had two lead singers, with Bruce and Clapton alternating lines in the verse and singing harmony together in the chorus.

The song begins with the guitar and bass for the first 2 bars, which are then joined by the drums for the next 2 bars. Unlike a common pop song, it doesn't feature a signature hook since the bass/guitar riff line is a hook in itself. The interlude is just 2 bars of the verse, and also does not feature a true hook or melody on top of the song's foundation elements. The end of the final verse features an additional 2 bars with the vocals of bassist Jack Bruce and guitarist Eric Clapton answering each other.

Arrangement Elements
The Foundation: Drums
The Rhythm: Guitar and bass (they play the same riff)
The Pad: None
The Lead: Vocals, guitar solo
The Fills: Guitar

This is one of those rare songs that only has three arrangement elements occurring at the same time throughout the song. The vast majority of songs may have three elements for a portion of the song, but eventually graduate to four or even five. (You'll almost never have more than five simultaneous elements since that just confuses the listener, and breaks a basic arrangement rule of having too many elements occurring at once.)

THE SOUND

"Sunshine of Your Love" was recorded by the legendary Tom Dowd at Atlantic Studios in New York City. As with most songs of the era, it's clean, not very compressed, and not very loud, especially when compared with the songs of today. It also doesn't have much low end on the mix, since that wasn't much of a priority at the time—mostly because no one had the speakers at home to reproduce it anyway. Engineering emphasis of the bass frequencies began during the 1970s.

The stereo panning is typical 1967, with the drums on the right side and the rhythm guitar on the left. Take note of the long delayed reverb that's prominent on the vocals, and a little less so on the guitar. The drums, in turn, are pretty dry.

Jack Bruce's bass is pretty distorted and the amp is obviously miked. There was no such thing as "going direct" back in those days. In fact, direct boxes didn't even become a standard studio device until another 10 years after this track was cut.

Bruce's vocal is also distorted, especially when he really opens up on the B sections. It has just a touch of reverb, and you can hear the compressor grabbing a bit, but it's not a bad sound in general. Also, listen to all the breath noise in the vocal. If the song was recorded today, that would probably be eliminated, but it does give the vocal a sense of realism and character. Also listen to how Bruce's and Clapton's vocals are slightly split in the stereo field during the choruses.

Of particular interest is the sound of the guitar solo, which Clapton called his "Woman Tone," and came from his 1964 Gibson SG guitar played through a Marshall JTM 100 Model 1957 "Super Lead" amp head and matching 4 x 12 cabinet. Clapton has explained that the sound was a result of the tone control of the guitar's neck pickup set to full "off" and the bass, middle, and treble controls on the amp set to max.

◀)) **Listen Up**
To the delayed reverb at the end of each vocal phrase.
To the breaths between the vocal phrases.

THE PRODUCTION

Back in 1967, production consisted more of getting everyone to the studio on time, keeping everyone inspired, and choosing the correct take, which is something that producer Felix Pappalardi did well in this case.

There is one production piece that was crucial to the song though, by way of engineer Dowd, who later went on to a successful career as a producer. After the band struggled to get a handle on the song, he suggested that drummer Ginger Baker use the American Indian beat heard in so many western movies at the time. Although the beat wasn't the norm for rock then and still isn't today, it made "Sunshine" come to life to go on to become the breakthrough hit for the band.

The drum part he's referring to is exceptionally unusual since it revolves around Ginger Baker's toms emphasizing beats 1 and 3 instead of 2 and 4 like on most songs, which is sometimes called a "backwards drumbeat" by drummers. There's very little snare drum and the only time you hear cymbals is in choruses and the solo (although you hear them more as the song progresses). "Sunshine of Your Love" was very different for the time, and is still very different today.

The Rolling Stones
Gimme Shelter

Song Facts

Album: *Let It Bleed*

Writers: Mick Jagger, Keith Richards

Producer: Jimmy Miller

Studios: Olympic Studios (London), Sunset Sound (Hollywood)

Release Date: December 5, 1969

Length: 4:37

Sales: 2+ million (album)

Highest Chart Position: Not released as a single, #3 U.S. Billboard Album Chart

"Gimme Shelter" is the seminal opening track from The Rolling Stones' 1969 release *Let It Bleed*, which was a huge worldwide hit at the time. The song was never released as a single, but it's been a big part of The Stones set in concert and has been used in dozens of movies and television shows, as well as covered by a host of artists.

Although one of the band's most popular and revered songs, it provokes a rather dark mood. Jagger has since been quoted in many interviews that the song was a reflection of tension of the time when the song was written in 1969, mostly due to the Vietnam war. Because of that raw emotion, the song has since been used as a backdrop for many natural disasters, such as the recent Hurricane Sandy on the East Coast in 2012.

The basic track to the song was recorded at Olympic Studios in London with drummer Charlie Watts, bassist Bill Wyman, producer Jimmy Miller on guiro (a hand-held Latin percussion instrument), pianist Nicky Hopkins, and guitarist Keith Richards on the basic track where

Richards also sang a scratch vocal track. The song was later finished at Sunset Sound in Hollywood with the addition of Mick Jagger's lead vocals and harmonica and Merry Clayton's soaring harmony vocals. Stones guitarist Brian Jones, who was still in the band at this point, was absent from the sessions.

The addition of Clayton was a spur-of-the-moment idea from producer Miller, who was the one that called her in. She was still in curlers as it was in the middle of the night. On returning home, she suffered a miscarriage due to her strenuous vocal performance.

THE SONG

"Gimme Shelter" is interesting from a songwriting standpoint in that it mostly revolves around a single three-chord pattern that repeats over and over, except for the verse, which stays on the first chord of the pattern. The form looks like this:

intro | verse | chorus | interlude | verse | chorus | solo (verse and chorus) |
bridge (chorus) | verse | chorus | chorus | outro

The solo is played over a verse and chorus, with the harmonica taking the verse and the lead guitar taking the chorus. The bridge is actually just a change in the energy thanks to the solo vocal by Clayton, which is also over a chorus.

THE ARRANGEMENT

The arrangement of "Gimme Shelter" seems like there wasn't much thought given to it in terms of song dynamics except for the intro, but it still works out well.

The intro begins with a tremolo rhythm guitar followed by two excellent sounding tom hits, after which Watts plays the hi-hat against the guiro on the second time through the pattern. That's where the doubled "Ooos" enter, as does the lead guitar playing fills. The third time the pattern plays, the kick and bass enter very softly, then the bass enters playing the pedal of the key of the song (C#) at full volume over the fourth repeat of the pattern. On the fifth time around, the piano enters, also playing a pedal note on both the left and right hands, while the bass alters its pattern just a bit, sliding up from the flat 7th. The sixth time is when the drums enter with the beat and the bass begins to follow the chord pattern.

On the verse, a second rhythm guitar enters, but without the tremolo, and the piano drops out or is decreased in level so it's barely perceptible. The first and second verses and choruses are basically the same, with Clayton's harmony and Richard's lead guitar fills entering in the choruses.

Maracas enter at the harmonica part of the solo at about 2:00, while a guitar solo plays underneath, and is then featured during the chorus part of the solo. The chorus continues with Clayton's solo vocal part entering. Later in the song, a third vocal harmony (presumably sung by Richards) also enters on the chorus.

At the end of the solo, the harmonica comes back for a brief interlude, then the piano enters for the last verse and Clayton adds harmony to the end of Jagger's vocal phrases. The outro after the vocals features dueling solos between harmonica and lead guitar.

Arrangement Elements
The Foundation: Bass, drums
The Rhythm: Guiro, maracas, rhythm guitar, piano
The Pad: None
The Lead: Lead vocals, lead guitar
The Fills: Lead guitar

THE SOUND

As you'd expect, the sound of the drums is very '60s, as it's surrounded by a lot of room ambience since the kit probably was recorded with only a couple of mics. If you listen to the isolated drum track, you can hear the rhythm guitar leakage, which suggests that the basic tracks might have been only drums, rhythm guitar, percussion, and vocals.

One thing that jumps out is how thick and long the reverb on the vocal track is. It's also delayed so it stays out of way of the lead vocal a bit, but there's a lot more of it than there seems to be on the final mix. Also, notice how low the vocals sit in the mix, and how distorted they are, especially Merry Clayton's solo when she begins to belt it out.

◀))) **Listen Up**

To the maracas that enter at 2:00 during the harmonica solo.

To the three-part harmony on the chorus after the solos.

To the long delayed reverb on the vocals.

To the distortion on Merry Clayton's vocals.

THE PRODUCTION

You always hear stories about what a light hitter drummer Charlie Watts is (he's been known to go years between breaking snare drum heads), but that's not true in this song as he leans into it with some muscle. His performance is very solid with great tempo, especially during the fills.

The percussion provides movement to the arrangement that's subtle but really pushes the song along. This is a Jimmy Miller trademark and it's used a lot by The Stones during this period.

There are a number of "mistakes" that probably wouldn't have been kept had the song been made today, like the last note of the lead guitar fill right as the vocal enters in the first verse (it's a bit late), or Merry

Clayton's voice cracking during her vocal solo in the bridge. Actually, the crack really makes it seem a lot more human and paints the emotion better, but most producers today would never let something like that go by without fixing it.

Another thing to listen for is how loose the bass and drums are. Back in the days when "Gimme Shelter" was made, bands never concentrated on being tight the way we do today, going instead for feel. "Tightness" as we now know it is a concept that's been richly refined since then.

Clayton's vocal solo in the bridge is a great example of natural dynamics in a song where the performance itself is the dynamic factor. Her vocal is set up to stand out following the guitar solo, and it probably wouldn't have seemed as intense had it been after a vocal chorus, which illustrates perfectly how important the song form can be in the production of a song.

Frank Zappa
Peaches en Regalia

SONG FACTS

Album: *Hot Rats*
Writer: Frank Zappa
Producer: Frank Zappa
Studio: TTG Studios (Hollywood)
Release Date: 1969
Length: 3:28
Sales: Unknown
Highest Chart Position: Not released as a single, #173 U.S. Billboard Album Chart

Hot Rats, Frank Zappa's second solo album, yielded one of his most memorable songs, "Peaches en Regalia." The album was released in 1969 and was not only one of the first recorded using a 16-track tape machine, but one of the first to utilize stereo drum recording as well. Zappa also used a recording technique he dubbed "double speed percussion," which meant recording the drums at half-speed so when they're brought back up to normal speed they have a distinct high-pitched sound.

The song was written in 1969 for his newly born son Dweezil—and 40 years later, Dweezil repaid the tribute by winning a GRAMMY® Award for Best Rock Instrumental Performance for his version of the song recorded with his band Zappa Plays Zappa.

Just to demonstrate how well-respected the song is, "Peaches en Regalia" has been included in the underground version of the jazz jam book, *The Real Book*, despite being compositionally more complex than typical jam-session tunes. Having a song included in this book is often described as the ultimate insider achievement for a jazz composer.

THE SONG

How do you describe Frank Zappa's music? It's always been hard to categorize because Zappa lived in so many musical worlds. In fact "Peaches en Regalia" has a lot more jazz and classical traits than it does rock, and here's why. The song form is anything but pop or rock-like in that the sections don't keep to the normal 4 or 8 bars. In fact, there are a lot of sections, including some that never repeat in the song. Here's how the form looks:

> fill intro | chorus | A section (8 bars) | B section (10 bars) | C section (8 bars) |
> D section (9 bars) | E section (13 bars) | chorus | A section repeated through fade

The fact that the song begins with a chorus, which you hear only twice in the song, and the A section repeats twice, makes it seem like a familiar form, but it's far from it. Add to that the odd number of bars in some of the sections and you have a song form that's quite unusual.

THE ARRANGEMENT

Here's another place where there's more similarities to jazz and classical than anything else. First is the melody line doubling. You hear piano and double-speed guitar, flute and guitar, sax and baritone guitar, synth and guitar, and more combinations in one song than you might hear in an entire pop album. The instrumentation not only constantly varies, but so does the instrument arrangement roles as well, which keeps the song not only interesting, but continually so on repeated listening.

The song begins with a drum fill and bass riff into the chorus, which consists of a double-speed guitar and the piano playing the melody, with piano flourishes in-between the melody line.

The first A section consists of a baritone guitar on the left channel and a double-speed guitar playing the melody on the right, with a synthesizer also playing the melody in the center, but set low in the mix. An organ playing in the low register and also placed low in the mix glues it all together.

When the song goes into the B section, two soprano saxes play the melody line panned left and right, with a clarinet in the center. On the C section, the melody is taken over by a wah guitar along with doubled flutes panned left and right and a muted glockenspiel. In the D section the wah guitar continues to play the melody doubled and panned flutes play a counter line, then the organ (which sounds like a Hammond with the percussion tab on) plays the melody on the next section.

When the song comes back to the chorus again, the organ plays the melody line instead of the piano and the saxes replace the guitar. In every section the melody is played by a different instrument with a different timbre, which is one of Zappa's many arranging tricks that's well worth studying for any producer or arranger today.

Arrangement Elements
The Foundation: Drums
The Rhythm: The bass pushes the motion of the song
The Pad: Organ played in the lower registers
The Lead: Various combinations of doubled instruments, sometimes played in octaves
The Fills: Various instruments from grand piano to saxes, especially in the outro of the song; double-speed percussion in the second chorus

THE SOUND

At the time this album was released it was lauded for its high-quality sound, which is mostly true except that the drums are very boxy and small sounding, almost like they were either played too loud or really over-EQed during mixing. They're also very low in the mix, with the kick masked almost entirely in the denser arranged sections of the song.

The bass also seems like it was over-EQed on the bottom end, which was very common at the time when this was recorded, when everyone was still learning what worked and what didn't in multitrack recording. The horns, guitars, and piano all sound great though.

Surprisingly, everything is dry as a bone, with no reverb or effects added, which is contrary to most releases of the time period.

◀))) **Listen Up**
To the wrong chord that's played by the organ at 2:49.
To the way that the horns are doubled and panned left and right.
To the double-speed percussion during the second chorus at 2:20.

THE PRODUCTION

The performances are a little on the loose side, which is another way the song is very jazz-like. The horns sound very much like a traditional jazz record, where they play the head of the song or read a chart without much rehearsal. It's not bad, but nothing like the performances of later Zappa releases.

Much of production is arrangement, and Zappa was a master at it. The additional tracks that the then-new 16-track tape recorder offered allowed him to overdub many more instrument tracks than were possible previously, as evidenced by the many doublings of the melody line. Likewise, the vision to understand that having the extra tracks made stereo drum recording possible was way ahead of its time, but something that every recording shares to this day.

Led Zeppelin
Stairway to Heaven

SONG FACTS

Album: *Led Zeppelin IV*

Writers: Robert Plant, Jimmy Page

Producer: Jimmy Page

Studios: Basing Street Studios (London), Headley Grange (Hampshire), Island Studios (London)

Release Date: November 8, 1971

Length: 8:02

Sales: 32+ million worldwide (album)

Highest Chart Position: Not released as a single, #2 U.S. Billboard Album Chart, #1 U.K. Albums Chart

"Stairway to Heaven" was perhaps the centerpiece of Led Zeppelin's *Led Zeppelin IV* album, which has long been one of the best-selling albums of all time. Sometimes touted as one of the greatest rock songs of the 1970s, "Stairway to Heaven" managed to break all the rules for a hit song—first, by clocking in at slightly over eight minutes in length, and then, by utilizing different song sections with different tempos.

According to several interviews with cowriter and guitarist Jimmy Page, the song was a conscious effort to recreate a similar epic to "Dazed And Confused" from the band's first album. Page actually wrote "Stairway" in several sections and only weaved them together into a song as he taught them to the band at Headley Grange. As the band was rehearsing, singer Robert Plant leaned silently against the wall listening until he suddenly jumped into a run-through with most of the lyrics and melody in place.

"Stairway to Heaven" was voted #3 by VH1 on its list of the 100 Greatest Rock Songs. It was the most-requested song on FM radio stations in the United States during the 1970s, despite never having been released as a single. This, apparently, was a strategic decision made by the band's manager, Peter Grant, so fans would buy the album instead of the single—and that's just what they did.

THE SONG

"Stairway to Heaven" is one of the most interesting songs ever in terms of song form. Everything about it breaks the rules of what we consider "pop song formula," but that's what makes it so cool. Here's what the form looks like:

intro (8 bars of guitar) | intro (16 bars with recorders) | verse (20 bars) | interlude (8 bars) | B section (8 bars) | verse (8 bars) | interlude (1 bar) | B section (16 bars) | verse (16 bars) | interlude (1 bar) | B section (16 bars) | verse (16 bars) | interlude (1 bar)

That's just the first part of the song! As you can see, several sections are different length-wise. Now comes the C section up-tempo outro:

intro (4 bars of different time) | guitar solo (36 bars) | vocal (36 bars) | outro (16 bars) | ending

There are a couple of interesting points to note here. First of all, the C section intro has 1 bar of $\frac{7}{8}$, 1 bar of $\frac{9}{8}$, another bar of $\frac{7}{8}$ and a bar of $\frac{8}{8}$, which is highly unusual for a rock song, then both the solo and vocal are 36 bars each, or nine times through the pattern instead of eight. Once again, this is so much different than what you'd expect, yet it works.

The lyrics seem like just words and phrases strung together almost at random, but they don't feel forced and actually seem poetic. That said, just about the time you think there's a storyline you can follow, a non sequitur pops up. For decades the song has made people wonder what exactly is a "bustle in your hedgerow."

THE ARRANGEMENT

The arrangement for "Stairway to Heaven" is brilliant in that there are only seven instruments, yet it sounds like a much larger ensemble.

The beginning of the song is mostly acoustic guitar and recorders played by bassist John Paul Jones. A Fender Rhodes electric piano holds down the bass from the first B section onwards to the C section. On the fourth verse, the drums and bass enter, along with a 12-string electric. An electric guitar then doubles the riff during the interludes. Take notice that the electric piano continues to play even after the bass enters, with the bass mostly (but not always) doubling it.

The C-section outro is built around the 12-string electric, bass, and drums, and the Telecaster electric solo on top is one of Page's best solos on record. On the seventh time through the pattern, a slide guitar enters with a line that answers the solo electric guitar. When the vocal enters it's back to the bass, drums, and 12-string, with the Telecaster playing an answer line on the third time through the pattern. On the eighth time through, the chords are accented by the band, but continue through for a ninth time (really unusual!). The song then ends with a solo vocal, which is, once again, unusual.

Arrangement Elements
The Foundation: Electric piano, bass, drums
The Rhythm: Acoustic guitar in the A and B sections, 12-string guitar in the C section
The Pad: Recorders during the verses
The Lead: Lead vocal, lead guitar solo, recorders in the intro and interludes
The Fills: Lead guitar in C section

THE SOUND

"Stairway to Heaven" was recorded on a 16-track tape machine at Island Studios in London as well as on location at Headley Grange, a large house in the English countryside, using The Rolling Stones' mobile studio. The acoustic guitar on the intro is interesting in that it's panned to the left channel with a somewhat long plate reverb that you hear more on the right side. Later in the song, the 12-string is pretty much bathed in this reverb.

The drums are heavily compressed, and are actually recorded in stereo. This, in fact, might have been one of the earliest examples of stereo drums, but it's a pretty mild version, with just a little of the crash cymbal and floor tom slightly panned to the left.

The vocal has a very short delayed plate reverb to put it in an environment, but it's still pretty much at the forefront of the band.

◀)) **Listen Up**

To the acoustic guitar in the intro panned to the left and the reverb panned to the right.

To the electric piano doubling the bass during the fourth verse.

To how the recorded parts change with each section.

THE PRODUCTION

Jimmy Page considers "Stairway to Heaven" his masterpiece, and he's not alone. That said, bassist/keyboardist John Paul Jones deserves much respect for his arrangement skills. The recorder parts throughout the first half of the song could have been boring if they were identically repeated with every section, but each one is different, which keeps it interesting.

The song starts quietly, builds to a crescendo, and ends almost in silence, which is an excellent example of tension and release. Listen how the instruments weave in and out of the track, even though the instrumentation and number of available tracks are limited. Remember that the song is 8:03 in length, but you still want to listen to it all the way through. That truly is the sign of a masterpiece.

Rod Stewart

Maggie May

Song Facts

Album: *Every Picture Tells a Story*
Writers: Rod Stewart, Martin Quittenton
Producer: Rod Stewart
Studio: Morgan Sound Studios (Willesden, U.K.)
Release Date: May 1971
Length: 5:16
Sales: Unknown
Highest Chart Position: #1 U.S. Billboard Hot 100, #1 U.S. Billboard Album Chart, #1 U.K. Albums Chart

The breakout song from Rod Stewart's first solo album *Every Picture Tells a Story* was "Maggie May," which eventually topped the charts in both the United States and the United Kingdom and launched Stewart's solo career. The song was originally released as a B-side of another song from the album, "Reason to Believe," but after DJs began playing "Maggie May" instead, the song was re-categorized as the A-side.

The song reflects a personal experience of a young Rod Stewart with an older woman. According to Stewart, the song is more or less a true story about the first woman, one much older than the teenager at the time, he had sex with in 1961 at the Beaulieu Jazz Festival. As is frequently the case with many hits, neither Stewart nor co-writer Martin Quittenton thought much of the song at the time of the recording and to this day are amazed that it became a huge hit.

The mandolin part featured on the intro of the song was played by Ray Jackson of Lindisfarne, who sued Stewart for back royalties in 2003 even though he was paid as a session player. Supposedly, drummer Micky Waller broke his bass drum pedal and had to play it with a stick, which is the reason why it doesn't have much punch. Ironically, the song was almost left off the album because the record label didn't feel it had a strong enough melody, but had to be included in the end as Stewart ran out of time to replace it.

THE SONG

"Maggie May" only has three sections—verse, chorus, and solos—but the distinction between the verse and chorus isn't very strong. The song form looks like this:

> intro | verse | chorus | verse | chorus |
> verse | chorus | solo | verse | chorus |
> | solo | interlude | outro

Stewart's record label didn't feel that the melody was strong enough, and while that might not be true, the fact that there's not much of a difference between the verse and chorus melody, and there isn't really a hook, makes their trepidation understandable.

The lyrics tell a supposedly true story of a jilted young lover, and while the storyline is strong, Rod makes little effort to rhyme, especially in the chorus. That's never bothered record buyers though, as millions of women everywhere suddenly felt they had some Maggie May in them. Interestingly enough, although Stewart sings "Maggie" in a number of places, he never actually sings "Maggie May" in the entire song.

The Arrangement

Much of the playing in "Maggie May" is very loose, and you get the feeling that they didn't do many takes to figure out each player's part. That said, there is a specific arrangement that works well.

Arrangement Elements
The Foundation: Drums, bass
The Rhythm: 12-string acoustic guitar, electric piano
The Pad: Organ
The Lead: Lead vocal, mandolin, guitar solo
The Fills: Electric piano in fourth verse

The song begins with an intro of a mandolin and an acoustic 12-string along with the bass playing a counter line. When the verse begins, the lead vocal enters as does the drums. While the drums, organ, and the 12-string play fairly straight, the bass never plays the same thing twice and is generally ad-libbed throughout except for the intro and interlude. During the chorus ("You led me away from home..."), the chord pattern changes but all the instruments are as they were during the verse.

The next two verses and choruses have exactly the same instrumentation, but the chord pattern does change slightly during the guitar solo. During the fourth verse and chorus, an electric piano is added playing random arpeggiated chords.

The next solo is the same as the first one, except that it's 6 bars long and plays bars 7 and 8 over the first 2 measures of the interlude. The interlude is the most different thing in the song as the 12-string drops out and is replaced by two mandolins that play similar (but not identical) melody lines, which is probably the signature line of the song. The bass also plays a more-or-less written line, imitating what

Photo: Neil Zlozower/atlasicons.com

was played on the intro. There's also a high organ pedal note that's doubled with an electric piano playing eighth notes. This continues for 20 measures (which is an odd number), and then the drums return as everything plays the same as in the section prior to the outro.

THE SOUND

The sound of "Maggie May" is fairly thin, especially the bass and kick drum, which have virtually no bottom end to them. Although not all of Stewart's band The Faces played on the album, this was generally the sound of the band throughout its life.

The panning is odd, with the drums panned hard to the left and the bass hard to the right. The intro and interlude have two mandolins that are spread slightly left and right, while everything else is panned to the center.

The song is bone dry, proving that hit records can be made without any effects whatsoever. Rod Stewart's vocal is clear and not overly compressed.

◄))) **Listen Up**

To the drums panned hard to the left and the bass panned hard to the right.

To the doubled mandolins playing slightly different lines in the interlude.

To the mistake in the bass at :38 as it fails to follow the chord change.

THE PRODUCTION

Stewart was the producer of the album, but as was often the case back then, that probably meant more selecting the take and setting the song's feel rather than directing the band like it does today. Plus, you can't really say that he had a vision, since he, his cowriter, and the record label didn't think of "Maggie May" for the album in the first place. That said, history has proven so many times that what artists, producers, and record companies may not be in love with is just the thing that the public wants.

The Who
Won't Get Fooled Again

SONG FACTS

Album: *Who's Next*
Writer: Pete Townshend
Producers: Glyn Johns, The Who
Studio: Olympic Studios (London)
Release Date: June 25, 1971
Length: 8:32 (album version), 3:38 (single edit)
Sales: 3+ million (album)
Highest Chart Position: #15 Billboard Hot 100, #9 U.K. Singles Chart

One of the most iconic songs of a generation and a staple of classic rock radio is The Who's "Won't Get Fooled Again." It was the first single from the band's most acclaimed and successful album *Who's Next*, an album that has perennially been at the top of "greatest" lists worldwide. The song is always highly thought of as well, as it was ranked #13 on Rolling Stone's 500 Greatest Rock Songs of All Time list.

What really makes the sound of the record is what everyone thinks is an arpeggiated synthesizer but is actually a Lowrey Berkshire Deluxe TBO-1 organ fed into an EMS VCS3 synthesizer, which makes up the principal rhythm element of the song. The synth turns the organ sound from bright to mellow and back by using a low frequency oscillator to control a voltage controlled filter, a clever trick for 1971.

Although a seemingly political song in nature, writer Pete Townshend has felt that its message has sometimes been misinterpreted. In a 2006 entry on his blog, Pete's Diaries, Townshend explained that the song actually carried no intentional political message, instead outlining the fact that a revolution can result in consequences no one can predict; and that today's militants are tomorrow's bureaucrats.

THE SONG

"Won't Get Fooled Again" has an interesting song form because it was built around a tape recording of the rhythmic organ part, so all the sections of the song had to fit within how that part was originally played. The form looks like this:

intro (synth) | intro (band) | verse | chorus | intro | verse | chorus | interlude | bridge | solo (B section) | intro | verse | chorus | intro | solo | interlude (synth) | drum solo intro | outro | end

The lyrics are typical Townshend in that they're well crafted and tell a story. In this case it's a political warning that the revolutionaries of today become the establishment of tomorrow, a theme that's just as appropriate today as it was in 1971.

THE ARRANGEMENT

"Won't Get Fooled Again" is basically the drums, bass, and guitar of The Who augmented by an additional acoustic guitar part and the rhythmic organ. The song begins with the band hitting a big chord, and the organ plays by itself as the first intro until the band comes back in with the second intro. For the most part, the instrumentation stays the same throughout the song with the drums, bass, electric guitar, an acoustic guitar panned left, and the organ panned right.

The chorus adds Townshend's harmony vocal, which is doubled, then it's reintroduced again during the bridge.

In the interlude before the bridge, the acoustic plays a double-time feel and is joined by handclaps, then during the bridge the acoustic changes from a strummed part to single notes, but changes back to strums for the rest of the song after that.

At points during the song you sometimes hear an additional electric guitar, but it's most prominent during the solo after the bridge, where both leads are played slightly differently.

Finally, at the very end of the song, Roger Daltrey's scream is doubled, as are the final lyrics during the outro.

Arrangement Elements
The Foundation: Bass, drums, acoustic guitar
The Rhythm: The modified organ sound
The Pad: None
The Lead: Lead vocal, guitar solo, drum solo
The Fills: Lead guitar

THE SOUND

It's hard to believe that "Won't Get Fooled Again" was recorded on only an 8-track tape recorder, but the great sound speaks to the quality of the electronics and recording techniques back then. Even though the track count was limited, the stereo soundfield is well utilized. The drums are recorded in stereo, while the acoustic guitar is panned hard left and the organ is panned hard right. When the handclaps enter, they're panned on the left as well. Everything else is panned to the center.

The electric guitar was recorded with its own reverb, which is different from what's on the rest of the track. The organ, drums, and vocals have a delayed reverb with a long decay, which wasn't timed to the track. You can hear this distinctly during the intro when only the organ is playing, as the reverb on the left channel is almost fighting the organ. Luckily the sound of the reverb is pretty good, so it never gets in the way.

The track is littered with popped "P"s on the lead vocal (called plosives), especially on the last verse whenever Daltry sings "parting."

The drum sound is a departure for the time as they feel like they're close to the listener, especially the toms. It almost seems like the toms were close-miked as we do it today, although that wasn't engineer/producer Glyn Johns' or The Who's recording style at the time.

🔊 **Listen Up**

To the synth on the right and reverb on the left during the intro.

To the background noise during synth solo.

To Keith Moon missing the drum and hitting his stick at around 1:20.

To the acoustic guitar at the end of the solo before the synth solo, and again right before ending.

To how the band is slightly out of time right before the outro after the scream.

To the bass and guitar change their rhythmic pattern on the outro.

The Production

One of the things that's especially great about "Won't Get Fooled Again" is the energy, and that's a result of the band playing with abandon. Back in 1971 production was less of a science than it is today, where most bands and producers weren't even aware of playing precision in most recordings. As a result, there are a lot of things that most producers (even artists like The Who themselves) would just never let go by without fixing today.

For example, both the acoustic and the electric guitars sometimes feel that they don't have a set part to play, and as a result, some parts of the song aren't played with real conviction. Sometimes the rhythms between the guitars are off, especially at the ends of phrases, and at times there are some parts a bit out of tune. The bass is the same way, where there's clearly never a true part to play until the outro.

Then there's the drums. Keith Moon may have been the most unique rock drummer of all time. His style is so different that no one has ever come close to duplicating it. Much of his playing on this song seems somewhat ad-libbed, but there's a method to his madness. As odd as his beat sometimes is, he is fairly disciplined at keeping it. The tempo is pretty steady, but much of that is because he was listening to the sequenced synth as a guide. Still, not many drummers were experienced at doing that back then. Occasionally he's on top of the beat a little, but manages to pull it back after a bar or so. That said, it's the fills that really set Moony apart. They often feel like a train wreck and are placed in odd places in the song, but it imparts an energy that's really at the heart of the sound of the Moon-era Who.

Nonetheless, there's not a producer on the planet that would stand for his playing style if he were just starting out today, which is a shame. How did he ever come up with that beat during the solo? And the one before the breakdown at about 5:30?

Still, it's one of the most iconic songs of all time in rock, even more so considering that it would surely be recorded differently and, as a result, sound different today, even if the original band members were recording it. Producers and artists alike listen a lot harder to a performance today than they did back in 1971 when this song was recorded, and the little things mentioned previously don't get by anymore without being fixed.

But is this attention to detail really progress? People still listen to this song decades later because the performance is so exciting, whereas the life is frequently squeezed out of a performance today in the quest for perfection.

That being said, "Won't Get Fooled Again" stands as one of the greatest rock songs ever recorded, quite simply because it was and is outstanding on so many levels.

Joe Walsh and Barnstorm
Rocky Mountain Way

SONG FACTS

Album: *The Smoker You Drink, The Player You Get*

Writers: Joe Walsh, Joe Vitale, Rocke Grace, Kenny Passarelli

Producers: Joe Walsh, Bill Szymczyk

Studios: Criteria Recording Studios (Miami, Florida), Caribou Ranch (Nederland, Colorado)

Release Date: June 18, 1973

Length: 5:15

Sales: Unknown

Highest Chart Position: #23 Billboard Hot 100

Joe Walsh and Barnstorm's "Rocky Mountain Way" from the album *The Smoker You Drink, The Player You Get* is one of those quintessential rock songs that any band can play, but not many play well, mostly because some essential arrangement elements are overlooked.

Although Walsh had achieved some measure of success with The James Gang previous to this release, "Rocky Mountain Way" was the song that broke him as a solo artist, getting as far as #23 on the Billboard charts. The song was written by Walsh as a tribute to his new home in Colorado, having just moved from Cleveland, and is one of the first songs to use a relatively new device called a talkbox on the guitar during the interlude section.

Walsh claimed that the lyrics of the song came to him shortly after he moved to Colorado while mowing his lawn and admiring the beauty of the snow-capped peaks of the Rocky Mountains.

THE SONG

"Rocky Mountain Way" is really just a blues shuffle, but regardless who's playing the shuffle or how it's played, it's a feel that listeners really like. The song form is pretty simple in that it consists of only three parts: an intro/interlude/outro (which are all pretty much the same), a verse, and a chorus. Like all hit songs, it's how it's put together that makes the difference. The song form looks like this:

intro (guitar) | intro (guitar, bass and piano) |
intro (full band with slide guitar) | verse | chorus |
interlude | verse | chorus | interlude |
solo (over an extended verse) | chorus | outro

The lyrics have a bit of the Joe Walsh tongue-in-cheek humor along with some political commentary during the second verse, using a baseball analogy. They also rhyme well and the cadence is strong, making it easy to sing.

THE ARRANGEMENT

As already stated, "Rocky Mountain Way" is a pretty simple song, but, as always, the arrangement is what makes all the difference. Take notice of how the arrangement builds in the intro, with the song beginning with a single guitar on the left, then adding a double on the right, then adding the bass and piano, and finally adding the drums and the slide guitar solo.

There are a lot of dynamics at work in the verse as the piano drops out, the guitar plays only the E-A-G-E blues riff, and the bass and drums alter their playing so it's more open. Then comes the chorus when the slide guitar and piano re-enter and the bass and drums change their patterns again to push both the feel and the intensity of the band, which continues into the interlude.

The solo is interesting because the song strips down again. The Clavinet enters on the left and the talkbox solo guitar on the right as the rhythm section basically plays the verse feel. On the last 8 bars another rhythm guitar enters on the left to build up the tension as Walsh continues his solo over the chorus and outro (which is basically the same as the interlude).

It's all tension and release. Start quietly with a few instruments, add more and build the level and tension up, then mute them and the tension turns into a release. Level up, level down, level up again by instruments and vocals entering and exiting.

Arrangement Elements
The Foundation: Bass and drums
The Rhythm: Piano trills on the chorus and interludes, hi hat on the verse, Clavinet on the solo
The Pad: None
The Lead: Vocal and slide guitar
The Fills: Slide guitar on the choruses

THE SOUND

Like almost every recording from the '70s, "Rocky Mountain Way" is really big and natural sounding, and although it's compressed, it never sounds like there's too much compression. One of the most interesting things about the song is the use of reverb. You hear a little of one reverb that's panned to the right on the rhythm guitars, then another darker reverb just on the snare drum of the verse. This dark one is delayed and pretty deep and long, giving a sort of "Grand Canyon" feel.

There's also something happening to the vocal during the verses that sounds like an early analog delay or a 30 ips tape delay. If you listen on headphones, the live vocal is on the left side, but it's also on the right side as well, only with a lot less high end. When the song gets to the chorus, the vocal is doubled with a second voice, which is panned up the center.

One interesting thing to listen for is what sounds like a bass overdub at 2:03 where the sound of the bass changes for a couple of beats. This could have been a bass fix that happened later after the tracking session was over.

◀))) **Listen Up**

To the rhythm guitar double on the right channel during the intro.

To the rhythm guitar that enters on the left on the last 8 bars of the solo.

To the long delayed reverb on the snare drum during the verses.

To the vocal double on the right side during the vocals, and the added vocal in the center during the choruses.

The bass sound changing at 2:03 due to an overdub fix.

THE PRODUCTION

The art of production is making a simple song interesting, so you can say that Joe Walsh and Bill Szymczyk did that job well. This is basically a four-piece band (Joe Vitale on drums, Kenny Passarelli on bass, Rocke Grace on keys, and Walsh on guitars) with a few overdubs, but it's the overdubs and the change of feel that make the song.

The rhythm guitar is doubled and a lead guitar overdubbed, and how those guitars enter and exit the song makes it build. Same with the piano, then later the Clavinet during the solo. Of course, a lot of credit has to be given to the rhythm section, who push the song along with a solid performance.

Once last thing: Listen to how far behind the beat Joe Vitale's snare drum is. That's the perfect feel for this type of song (or any shuffle for that matter).

Aerosmith

Dream On

SONG FACTS

Album: *Aerosmith*
Writer: Steven Tyler
Producer: Adrian Barber
Studio: Intermedia Studios (Boston)
Release Date: June 27, 1973
Length: 4:26 (album version), 3:25 (single edit)
Sales: 2+ million (album)
Highest Chart Position: #59 (1973), #6 (1976) U.S. Billboard Hot 100

Aerosmith's breakthrough hit "Dream On" appeared on their first album, appropriately entitled *Aerosmith*. The song originally sold poorly during the first year it was released, but gained decent airplay at a single radio station in Baltimore. Airplay on only one station wasn't enough to get their record label (Columbia Records) interested in spending many promotion dollars, until the song was named #1 Song of the Year by the station's fans during a Labor Day marathon. That caused Columbia to become excited enough to reissue the song, and the rest, as they say, is history.

"Dream On" had a lucky life in other aspects as well. Writer and singer Steven Tyler had been working on the song off and on for six years. A major breakthrough came when he purchased an RMI (Rocky Mount Instruments) keyboard with money he found in a suitcase outside of where the band was staying. Tyler didn't tell his bandmates where the money had come from, and he continued to play dumb when the gangsters to whom it belonged came looking for it. Thus, the "suitcase incident" became part of the band's lore.

According to Tyler, the song has meaning to him that goes far beyond the music, since it summarized his hopes for the then new band in the face of press criticism after their first album was released. As with many hits, he never imagined the song would be a hit when he wrote it on the piano at age 17.

THE SONG

Like so many hit records, "Dream On" is unique in its song form, which looks like this:

intro (16 bars) | verse (12 bars) | B section (4 bars) |
interlude (4 bars) | verse (8 bars) | chorus (6 bars) | interlude 2 (7 bars) |
chorus (6 bars) | bridge (14 bars) | outchorus (10 bars)

Obviously this is not a song written to a formula, since it's so long before the chorus is introduced at about 2:05, and the bridge is the only section that actually contains the title of the song ("Dream On"). What's more, just about every section is a different length. The first verse has 12 bars while the second verse has 8. The second interlude utilizes the same motif as the intro, but it's played in the major key instead of a minor and is 7 bars long! Then there's the bridge (the high point in most songs) at 14 bars and the outchorus at 10, which makes this a highly unusual song form indeed.

The melody and lyrics of the song are both very strong, and these sell the song to the casual listener more than anything else. The lyrics are philosophical in nature, but tell a story that we can all relate to. In a few places they feel forced, but in those places they are important to the message, and singer and writer Steven Tyler weaves them seamlessly into the arrangement.

THE ARRANGEMENT

"Dream On" features a straight-ahead five-piece rock band, with almost no sweetening. About the only thing that changes during the song is the sound of the keyboard and the addition of the Mellotron in the intro and interludes.

The song begins with the keyboard on the left and a guitar on the right with the Mellotron strings in the center. On the second time through the pattern the bass enters, and the pattern goes an additional 4 bars.

When the vocal enters for the first verse, drummer Joey Kramer also enters playing quarter notes on the ride cymbal, while the bass plays a whole note on every chord change. On the B section the second guitar enters playing a slightly different pattern in the left channel, then during the first interlude the same guitar plays a lead fill.

The second verse is identical to the first, but for some reason Kramer stops playing the quarter-note cymbals for the last 2 bars before the chorus.

On the first chorus the keyboard is mixed lower and the left guitar is louder, while both the bass and drums now play their full rhythm pattern, but all go back to the same pattern and balance for the second interlude, which is played in a major key instead of a minor as the previous sections.

The second chorus is shortened by 2 bars with the last 2 bars having a guitar solo played over them. This leads into the bridge, where the climbing chord pattern is repeated three times with an additional 2-bar build at the end.

The final chorus is twice as long, and ends with the minor second "European siren" pattern at the end, which uses an organ on the left side and a more synthesizer-sounding keyboard on the right.

Arrangement Elements
The Foundation: Bass and drums
The Rhythm: The picking guitars and keyboards in the intro, verse and interludes
The Pad: The Mellotron in the intro, first verse and first interlude
The Lead: Lead vocal
The Fills: Guitar fills

THE SOUND

"Dream On" was recorded at Intermedia Sound in downtown Boston, a small 16-track studio that was later purchased by The Cars. The song is recorded very basically, which was the style of producer/engineer Adrian Barber, who cut his teeth recording hit records for Cream, The Rascals, and Velvet Underground during his time as a staff engineer at Atlantic Records.

All of the instruments are pretty dry and in your face except for the vocal, which has a very pronounced delayed plate reverb. This sounds like the approximately 120 millisecond predelay that comes when using a tape machine set to 7 1/2 ips in the send path to the reverb. There are also a couple of bad breath pops from the lead vocal during the verses at 0:52 and 1:44 that are left in.

One of the cooler aspects of this record is the wide stereo field, which always stays balanced even with the guitars panned pretty hard to both sides, the keyboard on the left, and the Mellotron up the middle. Speaking of keyboards, the RMI used on the intro had a very cheap piano emulation that sounds like a harpsichord, while what sounds like a very early all-purpose synth of the time provides the organ sound at the end, and the highly modulated synth sound on the right side during the fade out (you need headphones to hear it).

◀))) **Listen Up**

To the vocal plosive that occurs at :52 in the first verse and 1:44 of the second.

To the delayed reverb on the vocal during the first and second verses.

To the right channel guitar misfinger at 1:45 and 2:45.

To the change to the organ and synthesizer sounds at the song's ending.

THE PRODUCTION

The performances on "Dream On" are another example of what was deemed acceptable back then, but would never be accepted today. None of the instrument entrances to the sections are clean, with certain instruments (mostly the guitars) jumping out ahead of the downbeat. The lead vocal even falls out of the pocket for a second due to a late entrance at 1:58. All this was left in and not fixed, yet it never hindered our enjoyment of the song, which goes to prove that production perfection doesn't exactly equate to a hit.

There are a number of excellent production aspects though. The rhythm section of drummer Joey Kramer and bassist Tom Hamilton is particularly simple and strong. The drums are especially solid and disciplined, unusually so for a young player. The interplay between the guitars is also wonderful and well thought out. Joe Perry and Brad Whitford continue that exceptional interplay to this day. Make no mistake, that's not easy, and you'll find some great guitar players that can never get the hang of what comes naturally to these guys.

As with most hits, "Dream On" is unique in so many ways and still holds up well today. It has a number of flaws, which makes you love it all the more.

Stevie Wonder

Living for the City

SONG FACTS

Album: *Innervisions*

Writers: Stevie Wonder, Robert Margouleff, Malcolm Cecil

Producer: Stevie Wonder

Studios: Record Plant (Los Angeles), Media Sound (New York City)

Release Date: November, 1973

Length: 7:21 (album version), 3:41 (single edit)

Sales: Unknown

Highest Chart Position: #8 U.S. Billboard Hot 100, #1 U.S. Billboard R&B Chart, #15 U.K. Singles Chart

Stevie Wonder's masterpiece "Living for the City" is from his 1973 #1 album *Innervisions* and was groundbreaking in many ways, from its social commentary, to the synthesizer use, to the length of the song (7:21). Stevie Wonder was the first black artist to embrace synthesizer technology in such a big way, which led the way to the synth becoming a big part of R&B thereafter. The album is considered one of the greatest in popular music history, ranking #23 in *Rolling Stone*'s Greatest of All Time list.

The song became one of the few social commentaries that Wonder has written in his career, and stands as relevant now as when it was released.

It was influential enough that hip hop group Public Enemy later sampled a line on "Black Steel in the Hour of Chaos," a track from their 1988 album *It Takes a Nation of Millions to Hold Us Back*.

"Living for the City" went on to win the 1974 Grammy Award for Best R&B Song, and the album from which it came, *Innervisions*, won a Grammy for the prestigious Album of the Year.

THE SONG

The interesting thing about "Living for the City" is that it's really just a 12-bar blues, but the addition of an instrumental interlude and two additional sections make you think you're listening to a different song form. That's the genius of the song. The form looks like this:

verse | verse | interlude | verse | verse | interlude | chorus | interlude |
bridge | verse | verse | interlude | interlude | interlude | ending

Two additional interesting points about the song form is that there is only a single "chorus," and the bridge has virtually no instruments; it's all spoken.

The lyrics to the song are somewhat forced so as to tell the story, but fit perfectly with the spoken bridge. They tell of a young man who arrives in New York City, only to be tricked into transporting drugs, arrested, and sentenced to 10 years in jail.

THE ARRANGEMENT

Like all hit songs, this one develops and builds as it goes along. The first verse is fairly sparse with only the vocal, stereo Rhodes electric piano, and synth bass. The drums enter in the second verse and the lead line synth during the first interlude, which is doubled with a vocal. On the next verse, the bass begins to vary from its original line, then the synth fills enter on the next verse. On the second interlude, the synth lines are doubled.

On the verse after the bridge, the drums are much more active with fills, the vocal varies from the original melody, and vocal harmonies enter on the last phrase, as well as anticipations and accents from the rhythm section (which are all played by Stevie). This continues on the next verse, followed by an extended drum fill. The outro interludes have a lot more movement from all the instruments as well as vocal harmonies.

Arrangement Elements
The Foundation: Drums and bass
The Rhythm: Electric piano in the verses
The Pad: Electric piano double in the interludes
The Lead: Lead vocal, synthesizers in the interlude
The Fills: Synths, drums, vocals

THE SOUND

This is a good example of an almost bone-dry song, with only a slight bit of delayed reverb on the vocal. It's so slight that the only time you can hear it is at the beginning of the song when there's only the synth bass and electric piano playing. The vocal is a little sibilant and the snare drum is pretty top-end heavy, but neither detracts from the song.

This is also one of the first examples of a song using a synthesizer for the bass line instead of a bass guitar. Stevie proved that it could work, and many, many songs followed his lead thereafter.

◀)) **Listen Up**

To the doubled synth lead line on the second interlude.

To the delayed reverb on the vocal during the first verse.

To Stevie's aggressive vocal tone two verses after the bridge.

Photo: Photofestnyc.com

THE PRODUCTION

While the concept of the song is brilliant and groundbreaking, the way the arrangement develops is one of the best examples ever of how to do it. Considering that Stevie played all the instruments himself, and given the length of the song, it is easy to see why this is a masterful production job.

Also worth noting are the two verses after the bridge where Stevie is singing in a much more aggressive tone. This was accomplished by co-engineers Malcolm Cecil and Bob Margouleff purposely getting Stevie angry to get his voice hoarse by doing things that would upset him, such as stopping the tape from rolling and not giving him tea to sooth his throat. While this doesn't make for a better relationship with the artist, it does accomplish the goal, which is to get the best performance possible.

Bruce Springsteen
Born to Run

SONG FACTS

Album: *Born to Run*
Writer: Bruce Springsteen
Producers: Bruce Springsteen, Mike Appel
Studio: 914 Sound Studios (Blauvelt, New York)
Release Date: August 25, 1975
Length: 4:30
Sales: 3+ million (album)
Highest Chart Position: #23 U.S. Billboard Hot 100

Bruce Springsteen's massive breakout hit "Born to Run" is the title song from his third album of the same name. *Born to Run* was released in 1975 and so many of its songs have been classic rock radio staples ever since. This was the first album to feature pianist Roy Bittan and drummer Max Weinberg, who would become the backbone of the E Street Band, but interestingly enough, they didn't play on this song; previous E Streeter's David Sancious and Ernest "Boom" Carter played piano and drums respectively.

The first recording of "Born to Run" was not by Springsteen but by Allan Clarke of the British group The Hollies. Its release was delayed for unknown reasons and only appeared after Bruce's version became a hit. Another interesting bit of trivia is that the recording was engineered by Jimmy Iovine, who would later go on to become a powerful record executive at Universal Music Group and cofounder (along with Andre "Dr. Dre" Young) of Beats Electronics, a producer of audio products and equipment.

According to all accounts the song and the album were a last-ditch effort for Springsteen to break through commercially. His previous two albums met with much critical acclaim but garnered few sales. The recording of "Born to Run" was done between touring breaks in 1974, well in advance of the album's recording. A prerelease was critical to the song's huge success. A mix that was different than the official version was given to the progressive rock station WMMR in Philadelphia, and it was then shared with WNEW in New York, WMMS in Cleveland, and WBCN in Boston. These core stations then began playing songs from Springsteen's previous albums, all the while building anticipation for the new release. With a major marketing effort by Columbia Records, it didn't take much to push the single and the album over the top. The ensuing buzz led to covers on both *Time* and *Newsweek* magazines, which was unprecedented at the time and the last push over the top to superstardom.

THE SONG

"Born to Run" is one of the most unusual song forms you'll ever see from either a rock song or a Top 40 hit as it fits none of the traditional formulas. The form looks like this:

chorus | verse | B section | chorus | verse | B section |
| chorus | solo bridge 1 | bridge 2 | verse |
B section | chorus | chorus

The chorus is actually instrumental, as is the hook. The song title "Born to Run" only pops up at the end of the B sections, which are an usual 14 bars long. What's more, there are two parts to the bridge, and it's really long, with the first part at 14 bars and the second an unusual 17. The solo is also an odd 12 bars in length. Not that it matters, the song just makes you want to keep listening.

The melody of "Born to Run" isn't special in that it's very simple with a lot of repeated steps, but that's not what makes the song special. The lyrics are pure poetry that fit so well with the music. Although a few of the lyrics break the cadence (listen to the end of the last verse), Springsteen sings them so they never sound forced.

THE ARRANGEMENT

Reportedly Springsteen was going for a Phil Spector-like "Wall of Sound" and that's exactly what he got. The arrangement is very thick with a lot going on, but like most great songs, it can be broken down into five or fewer elements. Let's take a look.

The song begins with a snare drum fill with the bass sliding down from the turnaround chords. The beginning chorus features the tremolo guitar playing the lead line doubled with a glockenspiel panned to the right channel, an organ playing 8th notes, the sax playing whole notes, a guitar playing a long strum on the downbeat of the chord changes, and the bass and drums.

For the first verse, a guitar doubles the bass and an organ plays in the high registers (but it's placed very low in the mix), which leads to the B section where the sax reenters, as does the glock (this time playing a different line), while a guitar plays a harmony line to the glock. The second chorus is identical to the first.

The second verse changes only in that the organ enters more prominently halfway through. The second B section is also the same except that a piano doubles the glock, and the third chorus is identical to ones previous.

The solo is a completely different section that, although it has the same instrumentation as the previous section, changes the feel, the chord pattern, and the intensity, which builds to a peak at the end. The bridge that follows lowers in intensity, with the glock playing a line that's doubled with a wah guitar. Halfway through, another guitar and the piano enter doubling the glock line, while the sax enters playing whole notes.

On the second half of the bridge a string section enters, although it's low in the mix, and the song builds to its peak. The last verse continues with the chorus guitar line doubled by the strings. The end of the B section builds tension by repeating three times, which leads to the last chorus and the big finish. All in all, it's an epic arrangement.

Arrangement Elements
The Foundation: Bass and drums
The Rhythm: A strummed guitar low in the mix and the organ playing 8th notes on the intros and B sections
The Pad: Sometimes it's the organ, sometimes it's the sax (like in the intro and B sections), sometimes it's a guitar playing power chords
The Lead: Springsteen's vocals, the sax solo, the tremolo guitar doubled with a glock on the intros
The Fills: There are no fills, but lots of counter lines played by the glock, piano and guitar

A couple of things to listen for: Springsteen is very good about adding and subtracting instruments during the song to keep the interest high. Notice the entrance of the organ in the second half of the second verse, the wah guitar and sax in the second half of the first bridge section, and the strings and horns on the end of the second bridge and last verse (admittedly, they're mixed down pretty low).

THE SOUND

The year 1975 marked the beginning of the 24-track tape machine era and you can bet that all those tracks were filled up on this song. It sounds like even a few instruments were bounced together and lost some definition as a result. The snare drum is pretty distinct but the rest of the drums, including the kick drum, are not, but that was about par for the sound of the day. The bass is very up front, also the norm for the time.

Springsteen's voice has a long reverb that sounds like it was delayed by a 7 1/2 ips tape delay. In other words, it's really long (around 120 ms or so) but interestingly, you hear it only on the right side of the stereo field. The other thing that only appears on the right channel is the glock.

 Listen Up

To the bass slide over the intro drum fill.

To the reverb on the vocal that appears only on the left channel.

To the way that the glock and piano line is turned backwards at the end of the song when the hook is restated before the outro.

THE PRODUCTION

Aside from the great arrangement, the thing that marks this song is the energy. You can feel it reach out and touch you right from the very first snare drum roll. It's intense, and that intensity never lets up, only getting bigger and bigger as the song rolls on. Although almost all hit songs have the tension and release factor of instruments entering and exiting during each section, "Born to Run's" dynamics are more from the intensity of the band than from just the arrangement. When you add in the fact that the song peaks not once, but three times (including the ending), you have a tour de force that served as a blueprint for all future E Street Band records.

Boston

More than a Feeling

SONG FACTS

Album: *Boston*

Writer: Tom Scholz

Producers: John Boylan, Tom Scholz

Studios: Tom Scholz's basement (Boston), Capitol Studios (Hollywood), Westlake Studios (Hollywood)

Release Date: July 25, 1976

Length: 4:45 (album version), 3:30 (single edit)

Sales: 20+ million worldwide (album)

Highest Chart Position: #5 U.S. Billboard Hot 100

"More than a Feeling" is the hit that broke the band Boston into the big time. The song, written by guitarist Tom Scholz, was the first single from the band's self-titled record released in 1976, and it set a standard for rock guitar sounds that came afterwards.

The song supposedly took Scholz five years to complete and was one of the six that he worked on in his basement that eventually lead to a record deal with Epic, five of which eventually ended up on the album. The song was recorded by Scholz (who played all the guitars and bass), drummer Sib Hashian, and singer Brad Delp.

According to Scholz, the song was inspired by The Left Banke's 1966 song "Walk Away Renée." Scholz has often credited Delp's vocal as a major contribution to the song, stating the main guitar lick only became a song when Delp began to sing. That close communication between the two lasted throughout their careers in the band.

"More than a Feeling" eventually made it to #5 on the Billboard charts, becoming the biggest single that the band would ever have, and was eventually named the 39th best rock song ever by VH1. The album went on to become the second biggest debut album of all time in the United States, selling 20 million copies.

THE SONG

"More than a Feeling" uses a slightly different form than the normal rock or pop song of the era in that the B sections are instrumental as they transition into the choruses. The form looks like this:

intro | verse | B section | chorus | intro | verse |
B section | chorus bridge/solo | intro |
verse (with an extra 9 bars) | chorus | outro

The intros are just verses minus the vocals, and the outro is a chorus minus the vocals. The bridge is where the solo occurs and is almost like a different song with a completely different set of chords and feel. During the last verse the song takes a left turn with an added 9 bars that builds to the B section guitar line.

The lyrics are pretty good in that they tell a story and are cadenced well. They roll off the lips with no trouble and the rhymes never seem forced.

THE ARRANGEMENT

The arrangement of "More than a Feeling" is pretty classic in that it breathes with intensity pretty much where you expect it to, except for one place. The intro is just doubled 12-string guitars, followed by another acoustic guitar doubling the bass when the vocals enter, with the drums playing a sidestick snare.

The B section is unexpected in that it's a Les Paul/Marshall lead line that fades into feedback and reverb into the chorus, which has doubled big electric guitars, handclaps adding motion, and harmony vocal answers.

The second verse is pretty much the same as the first except the acoustic guitar doubling the bass is augmented with a clean electric guitar as well. The second chorus is identical to the first.

The bridge is interesting in that it's a lead guitar melody over a new set of chord changes, which leads into the third verse, where the drums drop out and the intensity lowers. This is brilliant in that there's a new 9-bar part that's tacked onto the verse where the drums and lead guitar enter and help the song build to its peak with the lead vocal and guitar wailing on the same reverbed note.

The last chorus is identical to the first two but it only plays once, where it repeats in most other songs. The vocal exits but the rest of the instruments remain on the fadeout.

Arrangement Elements
The Foundation: Bass and drums
The Rhythm: Acoustic 12-string guitars in verse, claps in chorus
The Pad: None
The Lead: Lead vocals, lead guitar in the B section and solo
The Fills: Lead guitar in 9-bar third verse build, vocal answers in chorus

THE SOUND

The sound of "More than a Feeling" is somewhat mediocre quality-wise, which is probably because the tracks were done on a 12-track Scully tape machine (that's a rare one) in Scholz's basement in Massachusetts, then transferred to a standard 24-track for completion at Capitol Studios in Hollywood. The quality degradation really shows in that there's not a lot of definition in the tracks and everything has a fuzzy edge to it.

The unique guitar sound is the result of a 1968 Les Paul Goldtop Deluxe into a Marshall Super Lead "Plexi" cranked all the way up, but padded down with Scholz's homemade attenuator. The real secret to the sound appears to be an MXR graphic equalizer with the 400 Hz and especially the 800 Hz bands heavily boosted. Scholz also used a custom-made analog doubler/harmonizer that eventually became his "Dual Chorus" product marketed by Scholz R&D.

Delp's vocals are doubled, but not that closely, and pushed back in the mix a bit. This is another case where those vocals probably would've been fixed if done today. The reverb is rather plain and has a bit of a "boing" to it that you can hear on the fade at 0:43. It sounds like an EMT® (reverb) plate that hadn't been recently tuned. That's the only reverb used and there appears to be a bit of it on everything except for the claps in the chorus, which makes them stick out from the rest of the tracks.

◀))) Listen Up

To the way the song fades in on the intro.

To the drum and clap patterns during the choruses and how they add motion to the song.

To the vocal doubling the lead guitar at the end of the third verse when the song peaks.

To the clean electric guitars at the end of each chorus as the tension releases.

To the way the drums play along with the guitar during the second intro.

To the way each drum fill is slighted boosted in level.

THE PRODUCTION

The production on this song (by John Boylan and Scholz) was state-of-the-art back in 1976 and is still hot even by today's standards. The use of extensive doubling (the 12-string in the intro and verses and electric guitars in the chorus) was unusual for the time. Even though bands such as The Beatles had used the technique 10 years previous, they didn't use it with the precision used here.

More than anything else, the discipline in the playing is really impressive, considering that the song was recorded in 1975. Each part was well thought out and executed to perfection (except for the vocal double in a couple of places). That didn't happen much back then, and it took about 20 more years before this became a standard production technique.

The dynamics of the song are also well designed, with the unexpected peak of the song at the end of the third verse. The intensity swings during the song, keeping the listener's attention glued to it. "More than a Feeling" is truly a very well thought out song in just about all aspects.

KISS
Detroit Rock City

SONG FACTS

Album: *Destroyer*
Writers: Paul Stanley, Bob Ezrin
Producer: Bob Ezrin
Studio: Record Plant (New York City)
Release Date: July 28, 1976
Length: 5:17 (album version), 3:35 (single edit)
Sales: 2+ million (album)
Highest Chart Position: Single failed to chart, album #11 U.S. Billboard Album Chart

"Detroit Rock City" was the third single from KISS's hit album *Destroyer*, and although it didn't initially go anywhere on the charts except in the Detroit metropolitan area, it eventually caught fire as the B-side of the single "Beth" during a rerelease a year later. Today, "Detroit Rock City" is still a KISS concert favorite, while "Beth" is... that KISS song with strings.

The song, written by producer Bob Ezrin and guitarist Paul Stanley, is about an actual fan who was killed in an auto accident on his way to a KISS concert. In 1999, KISS bassist and film producer Gene Simmons turned the song into a movie, although the premise was changed to a group of teenagers who'll do anything to attend a sold-out KISS show.

The band was still rather inexperienced in making records at the start of the album, and credit producer Bob Ezrin with teaching them how to perform in the studio. That said, Ezrin was frequently at odds with guitarist Ace Frehley for his lack of commitment during the making of the album, even to the point where he brought in session guitarist Dick Wagner to play some of Frehley's parts.

THE SONG

"Detroit Rock City" is basically a simple song based around a verse and hooky chorus, but is skillfully put together both to add some length and some interest. The song form looks like this:

intro | verse | chorus | verse | chorus | 1/2 chorus | bridge | verse |
1/2 chorus | solo | chorus | verse | chorus

The lyrics tell a story and rhyme where they have to. They're not too clever but they never seem forced in rhyme or cadence.

THE ARRANGEMENT

The song is cleverly arranged to make it more interesting. The intro is a combination of a harmony guitar line played with the bass leading into the chord progression of the chorus. When the vocal enters you hear the basic instrumentation of the band with the drums playing a double-time feel, the bass playing a counter line, and both guitars panned left and right and playing power chords.

During the first chorus, the lead vocal sings in the holes left by the background vocal harmonies (the opposite of most songs), while the guitar power chords are augmented by a low octave piano at the end, along with a reprise of the guitar intro in the left channel. What's different from most hit songs is that both the verses and chorus are mostly identical in instrumentation throughout the song, without adding or subtracting any instruments with one exception toward the end of the song.

The second chorus changes in that it's a half-chorus vocally, then modulates up a whole step to act as a bridge with the same guitar figure playing over it, then drops back down and ends with the chords to the chorus.

After the next verse there's another half chorus, then everything is muted except the drums for 4 bars, then a lead guitar line plays 4 bars, which is joined by a harmony guitar for the next 4 bars. When the next chorus plays, a third harmony guitar is added and only the hook is sung in harmony.

The next chorus has the vocals on the first half, then a 4-bar hole with a drum fill at the end, back into the chorus with the harmony lead line playing on the right side up to a hard ending with a high guitar and low piano note.

Arrangement Elements
The Foundation: Drums
The Rhythm: Bass
The Pad: Power guitar chords
The Lead: Lead vocal, guitar line in bridge
The Fills: Background vocals in the chorus

THE SOUND

The sound is state-of-the-art for that period in time (1976). The lead vocal is doubled, but singer Paul Stanley does an exceptional job because the double is so close to the lead vocal that it almost doesn't sound like a double at all. The vocal also has a short regenerated delay and very bright long reverb on it. Stanley has a pretty dynamic voice, and you can sometimes hear the compressor flattening it out as a result, but it doesn't sound too bad in the track.

Both the drums (especially the toms) and the lead guitar lines have a long reverb on them, probably the same one as on the vocal.

Photo: Neil Zlozower/atlasicons.com

◀))) Listen Up

To the reprise of the guitar in the left speaker at the end of the first chorus at :51.

To how apparent the vocal double becomes in the chorus at around 2:10.

To the low piano note at the end of the choruses.

THE PRODUCTION

"Detroit Rock City" is a great production job by Ezrin, not so much for how good it is but for how bad it could have been. Just about all the instrumental parts are shaky, as they're not very precise in their articulations, and certainly not as good as the band would become in later years. As a result of the performances, the song just doesn't have much of a groove, although everything has a steady tempo. Still, several million kids at the time could care less, and loved the song anyway.

Where the band does shine is with the vocals. The lead vocals by Paul Stanley are spot on, especially the double, and Stanley, bassist Gene Simmons, and drummer Peter Criss have always blended very well together. In this case, the harmony vocals on the chorus are very tight, especially the phrase releases, which is an unusual trait for the period. Chalk that all up to Bob Ezrin's most excellent production.

David Bowie

Suffragette City

Song Facts

Album: *The Rise and Fall of Ziggy Stardust and the Spiders from Mars*
Writer: David Bowie
Producers: Ken Scott, David Bowie
Studio: Trident Studios (London)
Release Date: July 9, 1976
Length: 3:25
Sales: Unknown
Highest Chart Position: Not released as a single, #75 U.S. Billboard Pop Album Chart, #5 U.K. Albums Chart

"Suffragette City" is one of the most loved songs from David Bowie's seminal *The Rise and Fall of Ziggy Stardust and the Spiders from Mars* album, but interestingly enough, the single didn't break into any of the U.S. sales charts. Even the album, which was a huge influence on so many American musicians at the time, didn't actually sell that much in the United States when it was first released. In fact, it was considered somewhat of a flop in the States even though it was a hit in the rest of world.

Ziggy Stardust was recorded at Trident Recording in London in 1972 before Bowie even had a record deal (he was being shopped at the time on the basis of an album he just completed called *Hunky Dory*). Although many consider this to be a concept record, it was like most albums are: just a group of songs that, in this case, seemed to have a common thread almost by accident (read producer/engineer Ken Scott's memoir *Abbey Road to Ziggy Stardust* [2012] for the entire story).

The song's lyrics offer a range of unusual impressions. "Suffragette" is a more or less derogatory term, first used by a London newspaper in 1918 to describe a woman struggling for the right to vote. The word "droogie" is a fictional slang term for "friend" used in Anthony Burgess's novel *A Clockwork Orange* (and in the film adaptation of the same name). Even the familiar English catch phrase "Wham Bam Thank You Ma'am," often used by famous drummer Max Roach, must have been amusing to Bowie since it found its way into the song. The phrase was also the name of a track from Charles Mingus's 1961 album *Oh Yeah*.

Bowie reportedly offered the song to the band Mott The Hoople, who turned it down in favor of his "All the Young Dudes," which became a huge hit both in the United Kingdom and United States.

The Song

"Suffragette City" has a pretty simple song form that looks like this:

intro | verse | chorus | intro | verse | chorus | solo | chorus |
intro | outro (C section) | outro

All in all, it's a simple song, but both interesting and energetic. The outros introduce a different song section that you can almost think of as a C section, with the second outro being a reprise of the first.

The melody to "Suffragette City" isn't much, but at least there is one and it's memorable. In fact, the background vocals may be more of a hook than the main melody or lyrics. Speaking of lyrics, Bowie has always had a playful way with words, sometimes stringing them together to intentionally sound good but mean nothing, or sometimes with very specific intent. He's not married to rhyme or cadence, which makes him an interesting writer, but nothing ever sounds like it was forced just to finish the song.

THE ARRANGEMENT

Like most great song arrangements, "Suffragette City" builds and breathes. The intro is big, with doubled guitars panned left and right, then gets smaller in the verse, then big again during the chorus, back down for the verse, and so on. The song culminates with the loudest most energetic part in the dual outros.

During the first verse the song breaks down to the rhythm section, with guitarist Mick Ronson's electric guitar on the right channel and Bowie's acoustic guitar on the left. The background vocals begin on the left side and Bowie's lead vocal is doubled.

The first chorus gets larger with the addition of an electric guitar in the left channel playing power chords and a piano on the right playing eighth-note chords. Bowie's lead vocal goes from a double to a single on the "Suffragette City" lines.

The intro is reintroduced and it's the same as the first one, but the second verse changes slightly with the background vocals now on the right channel instead of the left. The second chorus is identical to the first.

The guitar solo is played over a verse and it's doubled and panned to both channels. You can hear that both of them are played slightly differently if you listen closely. The next chorus is identical to the first two except it's twice as long.

The outros are interesting in that they take up a third of the song and are perfect examples of how to keep listener attention during a repeating part (in this case going back and forth between a two-chord pattern). The lead and background vocals change every time the pattern is repeated (every 8 bars), and the synthesizer enters halfway through the outro section as an answer to the lead vocal.

Arrangement Elements
The Foundation: Bass and drums
The Rhythm: Acoustic guitar strumming in the verse, eigth-note piano in the chorus
The Pad: Synth and power chord guitars in the B section
The Lead: Lead vocal, guitar solo, synthesizer line in intros
The Fills: Background vocals, synthesizer

Although the popular conception is that Bowie played baritone sax on the intros, outros, and choruses, the sound is actually an ARP 2500 synthesizer, programmed by Scott and played by Ronson. Bowie has taken credit for the "saxes" in a number of interviews, but it's unknown if he just didn't remember or was being coy about the part on purpose.

THE SOUND

There are a lot of interesting sonic elements in "Suffragette City." First is Ronson's guitar sound, which came as a result of a Les Paul into a wah-wah pedal set at about halfway, into a Marshall Major. That's the classic Ronson sound.

The panning of the drums are fascinating as the snare is panned half-right and the kick half-left. This is because the song was recorded on 16-track, and the drum kit was frequently recorded either in stereo on two tracks, or with the kick or snare on one track and the rest of the drums on another, or some other similar combination. Regardless, the drums were recorded far differently from the way we do it today with each drum on its own track, hence the odd panning.

One thing that's frequently overlooked is how prominent the acoustic guitar is on the track, pushing the song along rhythmically and almost serving in place of the cymbals. According to Scott, "I wasn't too into cymbals back then so I mixed them low."

Bowie's lead vocals are doubled throughout the song, going to a single vocal on the hook of the chorus.

There's only a single EMT plate reverb on the entire mix, as that's all that Trident had at the time. You can hear the tail hang over a bit after the last chord of the song.

Also take note of the legendary Trident piano pushing the song along in the chorus and panned to the right side. It was famous for its brightness, which was fantastic for rock or pop, but didn't work very well for classical music.

🔊)) **Listen Up**

To the acoustic guitar throughout the song in the left channel that acts almost as a hi-hat.

To how the "Hey, man" background vocals change from the left channel in the first verse to the right in the second.

To how the lead guitar solo is slightly different in each channel.

To how the piano goes in a higher register the third time through the pattern on the outro.

THE PRODUCTION

Like all records that Ken Scott has produced or coproduced (he produced *Ziggy Stardust* with Bowie), the production is typically excellent even though it was only his second stab at producing (*Hunky Dory* being the first). One of the best things about this song is the energy, which can be attributed to the fact that David made it a point to never let the band go beyond three takes, so the players were always on the edge (this is with no rehearsal beforehand as well). Another interesting production fact is that, according to Scott, almost all of Bowie's vocals were done on the first take over the course of the four albums he did with him!

The background vocals (sung by Bowie and Ronson) are worth noting in that they move in the stereo spectrum, first starting on the left in the first verse, then changing to the right on the second and doing the same during the outro. All these little things add up to make the song both exciting and interesting, and as a result, a classic.

The Eagles
Hotel California

Song Facts

Album: *Hotel California*
Writers: Don Felder, Don Henley, Glenn Frey
Producer: Bill Szymczyk
Studios: Criteria Recording Studios (Miami), Record Plant (Los Angeles)
Release Date: February 1977
Length: 6:08
Sales: 16+ million (album)
Highest Chart Position: #1 U.S. Billboard Hot 100, #1 Billboard Album Chart

The Eagles' "Hotel California" has become one of the most iconic songs in rock history, and set a bar in production and performance that many artists still try to achieve. It's the title song from the album of the same name that went on to sell over 16 million copies and was #1 around the world.

Although on the surface the song describes a luxury resort (the album cover photo is actually of the renowned Beverly Hills Hotel), the meaning goes much deeper. According to several interviews with drummer Don Henley, the song is about the many excesses of the time period, most of which the band was experiencing on a daily basis.

The song began its life as a 12-string demo on guitarist Don Felder's home studio 4-track and was dubbed with a working title of "Mexican Reggae." The first full version was cut at the Record Plant in Los Angeles, but it turned out to be in the wrong key for a good vocal performance. The second version, also cut at the Record Plant, had only a smattering of lyrics and was deemed to be too fast. The third and final version, with both the music and lyrics now more refined, was cut at Criteria Recording in Miami and was actually made up of the best pieces out of five takes. In fact, the master take of the song had 30 edits!

THE SONG

"Hotel California" has a unique chord pattern and an unusual song form for a popular song. The main verse chord pattern of Bm, F#, A, E, G, D, Em, F# isn't used much in popular music, although it is a variation of a famous Flamenco guitar chord progression. The song form looks like this:

intro | intro | verse | verse | chorus | verse | verse | chorus | verse |
verse | solo | solo | solo | lead line | lead line fade

The intro, solos, and lead lines are played over the same verse chord pattern. Take notice that there's no bridge and instead of another chorus at the end of the last two verses, the song goes into the solo and outro lead lines. As was the case with many songs from the rock era of the 1970s, the song ends with a long fade.

The lyrics by Don Henley and Glenn Frey were actually inspired by those of Steely Dan, whose vague lyrics they called "junk sculpture." Co-writer Glenn Frey has often remarked that the song was kept intentionally vague as an homage to the Dan's Walter Becker and Donald Fagen, who often used lyrics that didn't seem to make sense. As a result, the lyrics consist of a series of cinematic one-shots that can be interpreted in a variety of ways. That said, they are extremely well crafted, a trait that the band's songs are noted for.

THE ARRANGEMENT

"Hotel California" has an exquisitely crafted arrangement that features many layers and some major song dynamics. The song was originally cut with all band members playing together, then layered with overdubs from there.

The beginning of the first intro has one 12-string acoustic guitar on the left side with a second 12-string acoustic on the right playing a slightly different line, along with the bass playing whole notes that outline the chord changes. Take notice of the hi-hat roll that appears on the right channel at the end of the fourth bar (halfway through the first intro). Also, see if you notice a little bit of guitar noise that was left in the space at the end of the second bar.

The second intro begins with the addition of a long acoustic guitar strum which occurs every other chord, along with a new guitar counter line on the far left side. Once again, halfway through you hear light cymbal and hi-hat splashes emphasizing the downbeat of the chords.

The verse keeps the same chord pattern, but now the drums enter, the bass plays a reggae line, and a new electric guitar part on the right side plays reggae-style muted chord "chucks." On the next verse a harmony guitar line is introduced with each of the electric guitars panned to a different side of the soundfield.

The first chorus has a three-part harmony based around the melody line, with electric guitar fills in the vocal spaces, which is identically repeated on the second chorus.

On the third verse the harmony lead guitars continue and are joined by another 12-string playing a whole-note strum on every chord. On the fourth verse yet another guitar harmony line is introduced, this time in a higher register than the original, which still continues to play. The last two lead vocal lines are also joined by a higher harmony vocal. See how everything builds and gets bigger and bigger as the song goes along?

Photo: Photofestnyc.com

The fifth verse breaks down to the same instrumentation as the intro with the addition of the lead vocal over the chord pattern. On the sixth and last verse, the entire band is back again playing the same parts that they played in the fourth verse.

On the solo and lead-line sections, the same instrumentation continues as during the third verse with the addition of Don Felder's lead guitar during the first solo, Joe Walsh's guitar during the second solo, and a tradeoff between both on the third. On the lead line solos at the end, the bass changes to playing a single-note figure with the rhythms of the lead line solo, and the drums emphasize the last two notes.

As you can see, instruments are added as the song goes along to make it more exciting, but removed during the fifth verse, and then brought back again for the sixth. It's a great example of tension and release.

Arrangement Elements
The Foundation: Bass and drums
The Rhythm: 12-string guitar line
The Pad: Whole-note acoustic guitar strum on the second intro and third and fourth verses; second, third and fourth verse harmony lead guitar lines
The Lead: Lead vocal, lead guitar, lead guitar lines on the outro
The Fills: Lead guitar, counterpoint guitar lines

THE SOUND

In 1976 when "Hotel California" was cut, studios were not yet that sophisticated and there really weren't as many outboard effects as there would be starting in the '80s. This song goes to show that with a song that's well constructed, just a single long reverb can make it sound pretty good. You can really hear the reverb on Don Henley's voice mostly on the first and fifth verses when there are not many instruments in the mix.

At the end of the second chorus, the reverb is muted so there's silence for a beat. It's gradually introduced back into the mix during the fifth verse. The drum kit is dry, which contrasts against the rest of the instruments, which have varying degrees of reverb, although the effect never sticks out of the mix.

Everything on this record is pretty clean sounding and the guitar sounds (both acoustic and electric) are fantastic. Much of that has to do with great players and great gear, but you have to know how to capture it as well, and engineer/producer Bill Szymczyk does a fine job.

In terms of mixing, this is a dense mix at times yet everything has its place, most of which is due to the different sound between the guitars and how they're panned. Notice that all the guitar harmonies are panned left and right, as are the acoustic guitars, which are the backbone of the song. The 12-strings do get buried at times but that's mostly because they're not needed any louder at that particular moment.

Also notice how low in the track the vocals and the lead guitars are mixed. This was common in the '70s, mostly because that was the best way to keep the band sounding powerful in the mix. The other thing to listen to is how high in the mix the snare and hi-hat are, yet the kick and bass still remain solid, although they don't have the bottom end that you'd expect if the mix were done today. You can hear the compressor work on Henley's voice during most of the song, for example, at about 1:45 on the last line before the chorus.

◀))) Listen Up

To how low in the track the vocals and the lead guitars are mixed.

To how high in the mix the snare and hi-hat are.

To how you can hear the compressor work on Don Henley's voice at about 1:45.

To how at the end of the second chorus, the reverb is muted so there's silence for a beat.

THE PRODUCTION

The production by Szymczyk here is exceptional, since the dedication to perfection is observed without the loss of feeling. Just the fact that the song was cut three separate times tells you that getting it right was primary in the band and producer's minds, as was the fact that the final track was an amalgamation of many takes. The solos and lead parts were worked out over a two-day period, which is an enormously long time for that era in music when most recordings happened much more quickly. Still, all the excitement is kept and nothing ever feels labored, which is the mark of a great production.

Dire Straits

Sultans of Swing

SONG FACTS

Album: *Dire Straits*
Writer: Mark Knopfler
Producer: Muff Winwood
Studio: Basing Street Studios (London), Pathway Studios (London)
Release Date: May, 1978
Length: 5:48
Sales: 6+ million (album)
Highest Chart Position: #4 U.S. Billboard Hot 100, #8 U K Singles Chart

"Sultans of Swing," the song that launched Dire Straits to international stardom, was the first single from the band's first album, also called *Dire Straits*. The entire album was made for only about $20,000, which was mere chump change in the big-budget days of 1978. The song didn't become a hit for six months after the album was released (unusual for the day), and was a major hit in the United States before the BBC agreed to play it in the band's homeland of England.

The song was written by guitarist Mark Knopfler, who got the idea while listening to a mediocre pub band. As the group was finishing for the night, they are said to have announced, rather tongue-in-cheek, "Good night, we are the sultans of swing." The rest of the ideas for the song came from Knopfler's daily observations of people.

The title "Sultans of Swing" is full of irony. Alan Freed, the Cleveland disc jockey credited with coining the term "rock and roll" played trombone in a band named The Sultans of Swing.

Photo: Jeffrey Mayer / atlasicons.com

The original version of the album contained a shorter version of the song that omitted a bit of the guitar solo on the outro, much to the chagrin of guitar players everywhere, but the full-length version was included on the remastered version in 1996.

THE SONG

"Sultans of Swing" is a fairly simple form in that it has a verse, a short B section, and a chorus. The form looks like this:

intro | verse | B section (1/2) | verse | B section | chorus | verse | B section (1/2) | verse | B section | chorus | solo | verse | B section | chorus | solo

The intro is a total of 4 bars with a guitar lick as the focal point along with the bass, drums, and doubled rhythm guitars that are spread left and right. The verse is 16 bars long and leads into what amounts to half of a B section that's 2 bars long, then back into another verse. The next B section is a full 4 bars, which then leads into an 8-bar bridge. This sequence happens a second time, which leads into the first guitar solo, which is played over a verse and B section, which then leads to a chorus. After that there's another vocal verse, a full B section, a chorus, then the outro guitar solo, which is played over the chorus chord changes during the fade.

The melody on "Sultans of Swing" is somewhat limited and although it is memorable, it's the lyrics that stand out. They're the best form of poetry in that they tell a story and paint a picture, all the while cleverly written. Mark Knopfler doesn't get enough credit for this part of his craft.

THE ARRANGEMENT

There's nothing fancy about the arrangement at all. It's a rock band playing at its simplest and best. Most of the sections have the same instrumentation and are repeated throughout the song.

The backbone of the song is the bass, drums, and two rhythm guitars that are spread left and right. The instrumental chorus has doubled lead guitars playing a chordal line. During the verses, the lead guitar plays fills in the spaces between the vocal phrases.

There's also a very brief harmony that only appears on the hook line on the B section before the chorus. This only occurs on the last three verses.

Arrangement Elements
The Foundation: Bass and drums
The Pad: None
The Rhythm: Rhythm guitar
The Lead: Lead vocal, lead guitar
The Fills: Lead guitar

THE SOUND

In the late '70s, analog recording was at its peak and this recording certainly is a testament to that. Everything sounds completely real and unprocessed. The vocal and rhythm guitars have just a touch of reverb on them, but the lead guitar has a lot of slightly delayed reverb that pushes it back in the mix, giving the mix a nice front-to-back image.

The drum sound is on the cusp of the old school and new school method of drum recording in that it's clearly recorded on multiple tracks, yet the drums feel as if they were recorded as a single kit. As we cross over into more modern drum recording methods, so often it sounds like a group of individual drums, but you don't get that feeling here. The cymbals are very present in the mix, which adds to the old-school feel.

Photo: © Jeffrey Mayer/atlasicons.com

The drums are mostly dry, but there's a nice long reverb on the snare, which is also very snappy (it sounds like some under-snare mic was added to the mix).

🔊 **Listen Up**

To Pick Withers' hi-hat work at 1:30 and 4:16.

To the delayed reverb on the lead guitar.

To how the lead guitar plays in the spaces between the vocal phrases in the verse.

THE PRODUCTION

Muff Winwood's (Steve Winwood's brother) production is sparse but effective. It's just the band playing with very limited sweetening, but the song is a perfect example of how that can be just as effective as a song that's heavily produced and layered. The rhythm guitars are doubled and split left and right and the lead guitar line in the chorus is doubled, but that's about it. What matters here is the performances, and the band just smokes, especially drummer Pick Withers, who plays with solid time and discipline, and his great hi-hat work pushes the song along. Of course, Mark Knopfler went on to become a guitar god as a result of this song as well.

Tom Petty and the Heartbreakers
Refugee

SONG FACTS

Album: *Damn the Torpedoes*
Writers: Tom Petty, Mike Campbell
Producers: Jimmy Iovine, Tom Petty
Studios: Sound City Studios (Van Nuys), Cherokee Studios (Hollywood)
Release Date: January 11, 1980
Length: 3:25
Sales: 2+ million (album)
Highest Chart Position: #2 Billboard Hot 100

Here's the song that broke Tom Petty and the Heartbreakers: "Refugee," the second single from their multiplatinum classic album *Damn the Torpedoes*. The album was The Heartbreakers' first Top 10, rising to #2 on the Billboard album chart, and was the record that turned the band into a superstar act. The album's name, which was part of a World War II quote from Admiral David Farragut, came as a result of a long legal struggle during which Petty intentionally went bankrupt so as to legally detach himself from a new record label that had purchased his contract from his previous label without telling him. With the legalities settled, Petty was able to enter the studio and record what became his breakthrough album.

The music for the song was written by guitarist Mike Campbell on his home 4-track recorder, primarily so he would have something to jam to in the key of F#. The song proved to be unusually difficult to record, as the band had trouble achieving the right feel. Reportedly, guitarist Mike Campbell broke down from the pressure and left town for several days in frustration, but that break enabled the band to regroup and successfully cut the version of the song that became the hit.

THE SONG

"Refugee" is as perfect an example of a hit rock song as you can get. Its form is an almost textbook pop formula, and looks like this:

intro (with guitar solo) | verse | B section | half-chorus | verse | B section | chorus | bridge | solo | verse | B section | chorus | outchorus

That formula doesn't make it a bad song though. In fact, it's pretty well written, with a strong melody and hook. The only unusual aspect is that the lyrics to the last verse are a repeat of those of the second.

Speaking of the lyrics, they don't read smoothly, with what seems like forced rhymes and cadences, but Petty sings them well, which is what counts. In a song where the music is as perfect as you can get, you can see that the lyrics don't have to be up to the same level to have a hit.

THE ARRANGEMENT

As with most hits, the dynamics in the song are great, but unlike other songs, they're not only created by additional overdub layers but by real dynamic playing of the band. Tom Petty and the Heartbreakers have always been a great live band, and this song demonstrates why, as the playing breathes with the song, pushing it to a peak in the bridge and bringing it back down to a quiet third verse.

Arrangement Elements
The Foundation: Drums and bass
The Rhythm: Shaker
The Pad: Hammond organ
The Lead: Lead vocal, guitar in the intro and solo
The Fills: Guitar in the verses, background vocal answers in the chorus

The song builds and develops in a classic way that every band should learn. In the intro, the full band is playing with the lead guitar over the top, then in the verse it's just the organ and rhythm section with rhythm guitar strums every 4 bars. In the B section, the band gets louder as another guitar kicks in, and in the chorus, the guitars go back to what they played in the intro (but they're lower in the mix) and the background vocals answer the lead vocal.

🔊 Listen Up

To the shaker that pushes the motion of the song along.

To the stereo organ with the low speaker of the Leslie on the left and the horn on the right.

The sound of the detuned snare drum, tuned as low as it can go.

The only fancy thing arrangement-wise in "Refugee" is the doubled lead vocal in the bridge, and the fact that the first half of the solo is by the organ, followed by the guitar.

THE SOUND

The sound was state-of-the-art when it was recorded in 1979 and still is today. Everything except the snare sounds big and natural, and you never hear a compressor working anywhere, although the song is compressed. The snare is very EQed, with a lot of crispness added, and it's detuned so it's larger-than-life sounding, which works well for the song.

It sounds like only a single reverb is used on the mix and it's slightly delayed (although it doesn't sound like it's timed to the track) with the high and low frequencies filtered so it doesn't stick out of the track. This allows engineer Shelly Yakus to use a large amount of it without it being noticeable.

The Production

Tom Petty and the Heartbreakers are an outstanding band. They play together as a single unit with plenty of dynamics, and that's a shining example for bands everywhere. Rumor has it there were more than 100 takes of the song until they got it to feel right. The key to production is knowing when you've hit the right take or when it's necessary to keep going. In this case, it was a good thing they kept going until they captured the right one, because it turned into a massive hit.

Rush

Tom Sawyer

Song Facts

Album: *Moving Pictures*

Writers: Geddy Lee, Neil Peart, Alex Lifeson, Pye Dubois

Producers: Rush, Terry Brown

Studio: Le Studio (Morin Heights, Quebec)

Release Date: February 18, 1981

Length: 4:33

Sales: 4+ million (album)

Highest Chart Position: #44 U.S. Billboard Hot 100, #8 U.S. Billboard Mainstream Rock

Rush's "Tom Sawyer" is a perennial FM radio favorite and the first single off their breakout *Moving Pictures* album from 1981. The song is a part of the defining moment in the band's history when they finally rose to worldwide superstardom.

The song was written on a band summer rehearsal holiday spent on a farm outside of Toronto. Poet Pye Dubois presented the band with a poem entitled "Louis the Lawyer," which drummer Neil Peart then modified and bassist/vocalist Geddy Lee and guitarist Alex Lifeson set to music.

The band was initially disappointed with their performance of the song in the studio, thinking that it was the worst song on the album. That feeling began to change as the mix came together and they realized that it was in fact some of their best work. Still, the band was unaware of the massive impact that it would have on their fanbase, and their own lives at the time.

THE SONG

As with everything Rush, "Tom Sawyer" is complex and doesn't follow a standard form, but that's why they're so well liked, right? The form looks something like this:

intro/chorus | verse | B section | C section |
chorus | interlude | solo | intro | verse | B section |
C section | chorus | outro

You can dispute exactly where the chorus is, but the popular thinking is it's where the "Tom Sawyer" lyric is mentioned. Nonetheless, the song is as unconventional as it is interesting.

While most of the song is in $\frac{4}{4}$ time, the solo begins in $\frac{7}{8}$, then switches to $\frac{13}{16}$. It then returns to $\frac{4}{4}$ until the outro, where it again changes to $\frac{7}{8}$.

The lyrics are poetry set to music, instead of the other way around. There's no overt need to rhyme if it doesn't fit the thought, which is a whole lot better than forcing it and having an awkward lyric or cadence.

THE ARRANGEMENT

Rush's songs are fairly bare bones in that they're meant to be played live, so there's not a lot of obvious layering. The guitars are doubled and heavily effected to make them bigger, but you can hear how they effectively use only a single less-effected guitar in the first turnaround of the solo, then the second has the full guitar sound to change the dynamics.

Arrangement Elements
The Foundation: Drums
The Rhythm: Hi-hat
The Pad: Synthesizer on the intro and outro, high register synth in solo beginning and outro
The Lead: Lead vocal, guitar solo
The Fills: None

Rush uses synthesizers very creatively, from the Oberheim OB-X swell in the intro and outro, to the Moogish sound in the interlude and outro.

Also, the lead vocal is doubled in the C section, which differentiates it from the other sections.

THE SOUND

The mix of "Tom Sawyer" is as interesting as its song form. Neil Peart's drums are way up in front and the snare has a nice predelayed medium room on it, which you can only hear in the beginning when the drums are played by themselves. All of the other drums sound pretty dry. The snare is fairly bright, as is the hi-hat, which keeps the motion of the song moving forward. The kick and snare are well compressed to make them punchy and in your face without seeming squashed. The cymbals are nice and bright but pulled back in the mix.

Geddy Lee's vocal has a timed delay with a medium reverb wash that blends seamlessly into the track. The reverb also has a bit of modulation that you can hear as it dies out, mainly during the intro when the song is fairly sparse. Lee's bass has that Rickenbacker treble sound yet still has a lot of bottom, despite the distortion.

Alex Lifeson's guitar is doubled using a short delay and slightly chorused with a medium reverb wash for the huge sound that glues everything together. On the solo guitar the reverb is effected and then spread hard left and right. It also uses the same guitar sound as the rhythm guitar,

which is unusual, since solos usually have a different sound on most records.

🔊 **Listen Up**

To the modulation at the end of the reverb on Geddy Lee's vocal.

To how large the stereo synthesizers on the intro of the song are.

To the stereo effect on the Moog synth at the beginning of the solo and the outro.

THE PRODUCTION

Any power trio has to have great musicians to have everything sound big and cohesive, and Rush does just that. Peart's drumming is absolutely rock solid, without a beat ever feeling like it drifted even a microsecond out of time, yet still feels organic. The way he's placed in the mix totally holds it together, yet it never feels as if he's the one featured. As with most other hits, it's the energy of the track that pulls you in, which goes to show that without a near perfect basic track, it's difficult to keep the song interesting.

AC/DC
Back in Black

SONG FACTS

Album: *Back in Black*

Writers: Malcolm Young, Angus Young, Brian Johnson

Producer: Robert John "Mutt" Lange

Studios: Compass Point Studios (Nassau, Bahamas), Electric Lady Studios (New York City)

Release Date: July, 1980

Length: 4:14

Sales: 2+ million (single), 50+ million worldwide (album)

Highest Chart Position: #37 U.S. Billboard Hot 100

"Back in Black" is by many accounts one of the greatest hard rock songs of all time, and it's the title track from AC/DC's seminal *Back in Black* album, one of the best-selling albums of all time. This was actually the sixth album by the band, but the first without singer Bon Scott, who had died suddenly, causing the group to briefly consider disbanding. With the newly hired Brian Johnson as their lead singer and lyricist, and Mutt Lange (who had previously produced their *Highway to Hell* album) set to produce, the band was soon to reach heights that no one could have anticipated. What most people don't know is that *Back in Black* is the second biggest-selling album of all time, with more than 50 million copies sold worldwide (22 million in the U.S. alone).

The band was under enormous pressure when recording this album, and no one more so than singer Johnson. The band reportedly asked Johnson to write a lyric as a celebration for the departed Scott, as they were against anything that might be deemed even remotely morbid. Although the lyric that he created was somewhat disjointed, in the eyes of the band it seemed to capture Scott's life perfectly, and cemented Johnson's place in the band that remains to this day.

THE SONG

"Back in Black" is a very typical rock song form-wise. It uses mostly arrangement techniques to develop the song rather than varying too much from the normal rock song form. It looks like this:

intro | verse | chorus | verse | chorus | verse (solo) |
chorus | bridge | chorus | verse (solo)

As you can see, there's basically only two sections: a verse and a chorus. The solo happens over a verse, and a different guitar line with a variation on the chord changes of a verse is used to change it into a bridge.

The lyrics never seem forced in the song and they feel good as they are sung, thanks to their natural rhythm. They are in many ways a tribute to previous singer Bon Scott, not so much the tragedy of his death but a celebration of carrying on while honoring him.

THE ARRANGEMENT

In their typical style, AC/DC keeps this song as pure as possible with almost no overdubs except the lead guitar. First of all, listen to the turnaround between 8-bar phrases during the solos. It's still a verse, but it sounds different thanks to this slight change of bass and rhythm guitar. There's nothing added to the second verse to develop it, which is unusual, but it still works great, as do the background answer vocals added to the last chorus.

Arrangement Elements
The Foundation: Bass, drums, rhythm guitars
The Rhythm: Unusual for a rock song, the vocal is in double time to the pulse of the song in the verse so it adds motion
The Pad: None
The Lead: Lead vocal and solo guitar
The Fills: Lead guitar between the vocal lines in the verse, background vocal answers in the last chorus

The other thing that's interesting is the dual countoff, first with a guitar and then the hi-hat. Countoffs are almost always cut off from a song (they're the sure sign of a demo), but here it just adds to the live feel.

The Sound

The sound of this record is great: big, pristine, very real, and in your face, but there's a lot more going on beneath the surface than it seems. Although the record seems bone dry, the rhythm guitar has a long reverb tail that only appears on the same side (the right channel) and the lead guitar has a short double that's panned to about 1 o'clock of the rhythm guitar side.

Brian Johnson's vocal is doubled, but the second voice is not at the same level and instead is just there for a bit of support. The snare has a nice room ambiance and has an ever-so slight bit of delayed reverb added to it as well. Angus Young's solo guitar is overdubbed and placed up the middle.

Photo: Neil Zlozower/atlasicons.com

◀))) **Listen Up**

To the vocal countoff way in the background before the song begins.

To how far behind the beat the snare drum is played.

The vocal double being slightly different on the last mentions of the title in the choruses.

To how the guitars are actually more clean than they are distorted.

THE PRODUCTION

"Back in Black" is such a band-oriented song that except for a few extra parts for support, what you hear on the record is exactly what you hear live. To pull this off, the band has to be exceptionally tight during the recording, which AC/DC certainly is.

Listen to how disciplined the band is. They play only what's necessary, with no extra ghost notes, slides, or other things that you'll hear most copy bands play when doing this song. Also note the way the attacks and releases are played by the bass and two guitars. They're perfectly in sync.

Finally, listen how far behind the beat drummer Phil Rudd is, giving it that tension that the song needs to really work well at that tempo.

Phil Collins

In the Air Tonight

Song Facts

Album: *Face Value*
Writer: Phil Collins
Producers: Phil Collins, Hugh Padgham
Studio: The Town House (London)
Release Date: January 5, 1981
Length: 5:31
Sales: 500,000+ (single)
Highest Chart Position: #19 U.S. Billboard Hot 100, #2 U.K. Singles Chart

Here's a song that helped shape the sound of the early '80s. It's "In the Air Tonight" by Phil Collins, which was the first single of his solo career and the first from his 1981 album, *Face Value*. The song was written about the anger Collins felt after divorcing his first wife. It was originally offered to Collins's band Genesis, who turned it down because they felt it might be "kind of too simple for the band."

"In the Air Tonight" is fascinating in many ways, not the least of which is the fact that 99% of the lyrics were spontaneous and improvised. As Collins told Mix magazine, "I was coming from [the] Genesis recording and rehearsing history, where, sometimes we didn't know what the vocal was going to be doing when we recorded the track, because lyrics were sometimes written after the track was recorded. I remember the first principle I had for making my record was that I would get a voice down very quickly so everything else would fit to the voice. The lyrics you hear for 'In the Air Tonight,' I just sang. I opened my mouth and they came out. I never wrote anything down, and then afterward, I listened to it and wrote them down."

The single went Gold in the United States, and eventually rose as high as #2 on the Billboard Hot 100 chart, thanks to a heavy dose of airplay from the newly launched music television station MTV. The song is a staple of classic rock radio even today, and has been used in movies and television shows around the world.

THE SONG

"In the Air Tonight" doesn't have a traditional song form by any means, but its form is understandable after you realize that the song was more or less improvised. The form looks like this:

intro | chorus | verse | chorus | verse | chorus | chorus | chorus | chorus

The intro is interesting in that it's 20 bars long, with the first set-up part at 12 bars, then 8 bars of the keyboard pad. The song then begins with a chorus instead of a verse. There's no bridge and the outchorus repeats over and over during a very long fade.

The melody of the verse and chorus is the same, so it's just the hook and the arrangement that defines the sections. The lyrics are amazing if they were truly written spontaneously, but then again most writers know that there are times when you are just a conduit and the song flows through you. The lyrics have good rhyme and cadence and are very poetic, a rare combination.

THE ARRANGEMENT

As unusual as the song form is, so is the arrangement. Many of the instruments used don't play the role that you're used to them playing, such as the guitar, which is used mainly for sound effect fills.

The intro builds but not in the usual way. It begins with drum machine, and a distorted guitar enters at the beginning of the second time through the pattern. A low pedal synth enters at bar 9, the moving main synthesizer chords of the song comes in at bar 13, and a high pedal synth enters at bar 17.

The first vocal is actually the chorus sung over the same instrumentation, except for the distorted guitar power chord on the last 4 bars. On the first verse, the high pedal synth drops out, but enters again halfway through. Both synth and guitar fills that are low in the mix fill in between the phrases.

On the second chorus, a low vocal harmony enters on the left channel and a long quarter-note echo is added to the end of the vocal phrases. Halfway through, a high synth line enters as does a high unison vocal.

The second verse begins with a vocal vocoder swell, which reappears later. The second half of the verse has an additional synth pad enter along with a harmony vocal on the left channel.

The next chorus begins with a big tom fill as the drums and bass enter. The bass plays a sort of modified reggae pattern against the straight time drums. The bass line is also doubled with a synth playing a stereo string patch, which is panned very wide left and right. The harmony vocal on the left channel continues, but another on the right channel also enters. As the chorus begins to repeat, the fade begins, as does Collins' vocal ad-libs, while the fills get more numerous.

Arrangement Elements
The Foundation: Drum machine, drums (with no cymbals) on the last chorus
The Rhythm: Reggae bass line doubled with a synth string line, high synth pedal sound during the first and second chorus
The Pad: Synthesizer
The Lead: Lead vocal
The Fills: Guitar effects, vocoder vocal at the beginning of the second verse

THE SOUND

"In the Air Tonight" was extremely influential particularly for the sound of the ambience on the drums. This was the result of the Listen Mic circuit on the SSL 4000 console, which is a sort of reverse talkback so the people in the control room can hear the musicians in the studio talk to them. The Listen Mic circuit has some heavy compression built into it so the level between musicians close or far away from the mic can be heard somewhat evenly, and this is what gave the drums the distinctive sound after the console was modified so you could record it. Producer/engineer Hugh Padgham later recreated the sound with heavily compressed and gated room mics, and that sound was eventually incorporated into most digital reverbs in what we know today as "gated reverb." This was the sound that engineers tried to emulate for a decade or so thereafter, as the gated reverb drum sound became very popular and was used on many recordings of the 1980s.

The song was built around a then-new Roland CR-78 drum machine pattern (called "Disco 2") which is bone dry in the mix, and it represents the base layer around which the song was built.

The synth pad, which is the most prominent instrument throughout the song, has a short delay (less than 100 milliseconds) that's panned to the right to give it a stereo soundfield, while the dry synth sound is panned to the left.

The lead vocal has a very distinctive sound also thanks to a short (less than 100 ms) delay and a touch of small room reverb. It's possible that it's the same delay that's on the synth pad. In the second chorus, a second longer quarter-note delay is introduced at the end of each phrase. The vocals also feature an interesting use of a vocoder in the second verse.

🔊)) **Listen Up**

To the high pedal synth that enters at :42.

To the harmony vocal only in the left channel for the second and third choruses.

To the unison octave vocal on the the second chorus.

THE PRODUCTION

There are so many distinctive sounds in this song, but the production really makes it a hit. While one might think that the synth carries the song on a passing listen, it's really the repeating synth bass drone and the high synth drone in the chorus that add motion. These two are low in the mix so it's easy not to be aware of them.

It's also worth noting how the song develops. The second verse introduces the vocal vocoder, the second chorus introduces a harmony vocal with a long delay at the end of the phrases, and the last chorus and outro introduce the drums and the bass line, which is doubled with a synth string sound. Collins then ad-libs the lead vocal over the fade of the song. There's constantly something new happening throughout to keep your attention, even if it may be subtle.

One last thing: Although the sound of the real drums on this record would change drum sounds for a long while afterwards, take note that there are no cymbals ever played.

Glossary

4 on the floor A drum pattern where the bass drum plays on every beat in a measure.

A-side The primary side of a 7-inch vinyl record.

B-side The secondary side of a 7-inch vinyl record.

Airplay When a song gets played on the radio.

Ambience The background noise of an environment.

Arpeggiated The notes of a chord played in quick succession.

Arrangement The way the instruments are combined in a song.

Articulation The way a note or phrase is played or sung.

Attenuator A piece of equipment that causes a decrease in level.

Automation A system that memorizes, then plays back the position of all faders and mutes on a mixing console.

Autotune A hardware device or plug-in used to adjust the pitch of a vocalist.

B section See Pre-chorus.

Bandwidth The number of frequencies that a device will pass before the signal degrades. A human can supposedly hear from 20 Hz to 20 kHz so the bandwidth of the human ear is 20 Hz to 20 kHz.

Basics See Basic tracks.

Basic tracks Recording the rhythm section for a record, which may include all the instruments of the band, but may be only the drums, depending on the project.

Bleed Acoustic spill from a sound source other than the one intended for pickup.

Bottom Bass frequencies, the lower end of the audio spectrum. See also Low end.

Bottom end See Bottom.

BPM Beats per minute. The measure of tempo.

Breakdown When an arrangement is stripped down to only one or two elements.

Bridge An interlude that connects two parts of a song, building a harmonic connection between those parts.

Build Usually a one- or two-bar section of a song where the volume builds from soft to loud.

Cadence The number of syllables in a line.

Channel In a stereo mix, the audio sent to each speaker represents a channel. There are also mix delivery formats with four, five or more channels.

Chord When two or more notes are played at once. Songs usually contain a repeating sequence of various chords called a chord progression or pattern.

Chorus (in a song) The refrain of the song following each verse, which usually contains the hook.

Chorus (electronic effect) A type of signal processor where a detuned copy is mixed with the original signal, which creates a fatter sound.

Chucks On a guitar, 8th- or 16th-note chords muted with the hand so they have a very short sustain.

Clean A signal with no distortion.

Click A metronome feed to the headphones to help the musicians play at the correct tempo.

Clip To overload and cause distortion.

Clipping When an audio signal begins to distort because a circuit in the signal path is overloaded, the top of the waveform becomes "clipped" off and begins to look square instead of rounded. This usually results in some type of distortion, which can be either soft and barely noticeable, or horribly crunchy sounding.

Competitive level A mix level that is as loud as your competitor's mix.

Compressor A signal processing device used to compress audio dynamics.

DAW Digital audio workstation. The software application and hardware that allows your computer to record and edit audio.

dB Decibel, is a unit of measurement of sound level or loudness.

Decay The time it takes for a signal to fall below audibility.

Delay A type of signal processor that produces distinct repeats (echoes) of a signal.

Direct To "go direct" means to bypass a microphone and connect the guitar, bass, or keyboard directly into a recording device.

Double To play or sing a track a second time. The inconsistencies between both tracks when played back simultaneously make the part sound bigger.

Dynamics Whether an instrument or song is played softly or loudly. Songs that vary in dynamics are found to be expressive and interesting.

Edgy A sound with an abundance of mid-range frequencies.

Effect When a sound is changed or enhanced with delay, ambience or modulation.

Element A component or ingredient of the mix.

EQ Equalizer, or to adjust the equalizers (tone controls) to affect the timbral balance of a sound.

Equalizer A tone control that can vary in sophistication from very simple to very complex. See also Parametric equalizer.

Equalization Adjustment of the frequency spectrum to even out or alter tonal imbalances.

Feel The groove of a song and how it feels to play or listen to.

Fill A short musical passage to sustain the listener's attention between melody phrases.

Flanging The process of mixing a copy of the signal back with itself, but gradually and randomly slowing the copy down to cause the sound to "whoosh" as if it were in a wind tunnel. This was originally done by holding a finger against a tape flange (the metal part that holds the tape on the reel), hence the name.

Footballs Whole notes. Long sustaining distorted guitar chords.

Four on the floor See "4 on the floor"

Groove The pulse of the song and how the instruments dynamically breathe with it. Or, the part of a vinyl record that contains the mechanical information that is transferred to electronic info by the stylus.

Guide vocal See "scratch vocal."

Hard ending An ending to a song where the music stops completely.

Harmony When a part in a song is played (or sung) by multiple instruments, each playing a different, yet related pitch, which usually sounds pleasant to the ear.

Hz An abbreviation for Hertz, the measurement of audio frequency. 1 Hz is equivalent to one cycle of a sound waveform per second. The higher the frequency of the signal, the higher the number of Hertz, and the higher the sound. Low numbers of Hertz represent low sounds.

High end The high frequency response of a device.

Hook A catchy phrase either played or sung.

Hypercompression A condition where too much compression is used and as a result leaves the song with no dynamics, making it sound lifeless.

Intonation The accuracy of tuning anywhere along the neck of a stringed instrument like a guitar or bass. Also applies to brass, woodwinds, and piano.

Iso booth Isolation booth. An isolated section of the studio designed to eliminate leakage from coming in to the booth or leaking out.

Intonation The accuracy of tuning anywhere along the neck of a stringed instrument like a guitar or bass. Also applies to brass, woodwinds, and piano.

Key When music conforms to one particular scale. If a key changes, the music then uses another scale than the original one.

kHz Kilohertz; 1 kHz = 1000 Hz.

Layered mix When the different mix elements are put into different artificial environments by using effects such as reverb and delay.

Lazy fill A drum fill that wavers behind the beat.

Leakage Sound from a distant instrument "bleeding" into a mic pointed at another instrument. Acoustic spill from a sound source other than the one intended for pickup.

Leslie A speaker cabinet primarily used with organs that features rotating speakers.

Limiter A signal-processing device used to constrict or reduce audio dynamics, reducing the loudest peaks in volume.

Loop A small audio file, usually only four or eight beats (or measures) that's edited in a way so that it can seamlessly repeat.

Low end The lower end of the audio spectrum, or bass frequencies usually below 200 Hz.

Master A final version of a recording that is destined for distribution.

Mastering The process of turning a collection of songs into a record by making them sound like they belong together in tone, volume, and timing (spacing between songs).

Mellotron A keyboard popular in the 1960s that used tapes of recorded orchestral instruments to generate its sounds.

Mid-range Middle frequencies starting from around 250 Hz up to 4000 Hz.

Mix The final balance of a recording where the individual instruments and vocals are balanced, tonally enhanced, dynamically controlled, and effects may be added.

Modulation (effect) Using a second signal to modify the first. A chorus uses a very low frequency signal to modulate the audio signal and produce the effect.

Modulation (in a song) When a song changes to a different key.

Mono Short for monaural, or single audio playback channel.

Monaural A mix that contains a single channel and usually comes from only a one speaker.

Mute To turn an instrument or voice off in a mix.

Outboard effect Hardware devices such as compressors, reverbs, and effects boxes that are not built into a console and usually reside in an equipment rack in the control room.

Outchorus A repeating chorus at the end of a song.

Out of phase The polarity of two channels (it could be the left and right channel of a stereo program) are reversed, thereby causing the center of the program (such as the vocal) to diminish in level.

Outro The section of a song after the last chorus until the end of the song.

Overdub To record along with previously recorded tracks.

Overtone The part of a sound that give it its character and uniqueness.

Pad A long sustaining note or chord.

Pan Short for panorama; indicates the left and right position of an instrument within the stereo spectrum.

Panning Moving a sound across the stereo spectrum. If a sound appears to be coming from the right or left, the majority of the volume is panned to that channel. When a sound appears to be coming from the middle, it is panned to the center, or equally to each channel.

Pedal A sustained tone.

Phase cancellation The process during which some frequencies (usually those below 100 Hz) are slowed down ever-so slightly as they pass through a device. This is usually exaggerated by excessive use of equalization and is highly undesirable.

Pitch A musical tone.

Plug-in An add-on to a computer application that adds functionality to it. EQ, modulation, and reverb are examples of DAW plug-ins.

Pocket In the "groove" (the rhythm) with the song.

Power chords Long sustaining distorted guitar chords.

Pre-chorus A section of a song between verse and chorus sections. Sometimes called a B-section. Not found in every song.

Pre-delay The time between the dry sound and the onset of reverberation. The correct setting of the pre-delay parameter can make a difference in the clarity of the mix.

Pre-production A process of familiarizing an ensemble with the songs and arrangements before recording them.

Presence Accentuated upper mid-range frequencies (anywhere from 5 kHz to 10 kHz).

Producer The musical equivalent of a movie director, the producer has the ability to craft the songs of an artist or band technically, sonically, and musically.

Production The process of overseeing and molding the sound, the arrangement, the song form, and lyrics to create the final song.

Pumping When the level of a mix increases, then decreases noticeably. Pumping is caused by the improper setting of the attack and release times on a compressor.

Punchy A description for a quality of sound that infers good reproduction of dynamics with a strong impact. The term sometimes means emphasis in the 200 Hz and 5 kHz areas.

Record A generic term for the distribution medium of a recording. Regardless of whether it's a CD, vinyl, or a digital file, it is still known as a record.

Rehearsal A practice or trial band performance.

Release The end of a sound or phrase. See also Tension and release.

Remaster To enhance the sound quality of an existing recording.

Reverb The hardware unit or plug-in that produces artificial reverberation or room ambience.

Reverberation The persistence of sound in an environment that lingers after the original sound is produced.

Rhythm section The instruments in a band that give the song its pulse, usually the bass and drums.

Roll off To attenuate either end of the frequency spectrum.

Rushed fill A drum fill that's played ahead of the beat.

Scratch vocal A temporary vocal recorded during basic tracking with the intention of replacing it later (sometimes known as a "guide vocal").

Sibilant When a vocalist singing or pronouncing a syllable that creates a "sss" or "shhh" sound that is audibly louder than other syllables.

Snare A thin drum with springs or "strainers" underneath that create a "rattling" sound.

Snare strainers The string of springs on the bottom of the snare drum.

Song form The order in which the different sections of a song are arranged.

Soundfield The direct listening area.

Stereo When a recording is mixed as two separate channels to be played through two separate speakers (right and left).

Sympathetic vibrations Vibrations, buzzes, and rattles that occur in other drums or instruments than the one that was struck.

Tempo The rate of speed that a song is played.

Tension and release Building a listener's expectations and then relaxing them, such as dissonance to harmony, or loud to soft.

Timbre Tonal color.

Timed delay A delay where the repeats are timed to pulse along with the pulse of the song.

Top end See High end.

Track A term sometimes used to mean a song. In recording, a separate musical performance that is recorded.

Transient A very short duration signal.

Tremolo A cyclic variation in volume.

Turnaround A short transition part, usually at the end of song sections such as between a verse and chorus.

Vibe The emotional atmosphere communicated to and felt by others.

Vibrato A cyclic variation in tone.

Vocoder A type of synthesizer that uses the human voice as an oscillator.

Voicing The way the notes of a chord are distributed.

BOBBY OWSINSKI BIBLIOGRAPHY

The Mixing Engineer's Handbook 2nd edition (Thomson Course Technology)
The premier book on audio mixing techniques provides all the information needed to take your mixing skills to the next level. Includes advice from some of the world's best mixing engineers.

The Recording Engineer's Handbook 2nd Edition (Course Technology PTR)
This book reveals the microphone and recording techniques used by some of the most renowned recording engineers, including everything you need to know to lay down great tracks in any recording situation, in any musical genre, and in any studio.

The Audio Mastering Handbook 2nd Edition (Course Technology PTR)
Everything you always wanted to know about mastering, from doing it yourself to using a major facility, utilizing insights from some of the world's top mastering engineers.

The Drum Recording Handbook with DVD (with Dennis Moody) (Hal Leonard)
Uncovers the secret of amazing drum recordings in your recording, even with the most inexpensive gear. It's all in the technique, and this book & DVD will show you how.

How To Make Your Band Sound Great with DVD (Hal Leonard)
This band improvement book and DVD shows your band how to play to its fullest potential: how to be tight, more dynamic, and how to improve your live show and recordings.

The Studio Musician's Handbook with DVD (with Paul ILL) (Hal Leonard)
Everything you wanted to know about the world of the studio musician including how you become a studio musician, who hires you, how much you get paid, what kind of skills you need, what gear you must have, the proper session etiquette required to make a session run smoothly, and how to apply these skills in every type of recording session.

Music 3.0 - A Survival Guide To Making Music In The Internet Age 2nd Edition (Hal Leonard)
The paradigm has shifted and everything you knew about the music business has completely changed. Who are the new players in the music business? Why are traditional record labels, television, and radio no longer factors in an artist's success? How do you market and distribute your music in the new music world—and how do you make money? This book answers these questions and more in its comprehensive look at the new music business.

Bibliography

The Music Producer's Handbook with DVD (Hal Leonard)
Reveals the secrets to becoming a music producer and producing just about any kind of project in any genre of music. The book also covers the true mechanics of production, from analyzing and fixing the format of a song to troubleshooting a song when it just doesn't sound right, to getting the best performance and sound out of the band and vocalist.

The Musician's Video Handbook with DVD (Hal Leonard)
A musician's guide to making any of the various types of videos now required by a musical artist for promotion or final product. The book explains tricks and tips used by the pros to make their videos look professional, which you can do with inexpensive gear and not much of a budget.

Mixing And Mastering With IK Multimedia T-RackS: The Official Guide (Course Technology PTR)
Learn how to harness the potential of T-RackS and learn the tips and tricks of using T-RackS processor modules to help bring your mixes to life, then master them so they're competitive with any major label release.

The Touring Musician's Handbook with DVD (Hal Leonard)
This handbook covers all you need to know as a touring musician, whether you're a sideman, solo performer, or member of a band. As a bonus, individual touring guides for guitarists, bassists, drummers, vocalists, keyboard players, horn players, and string players as well as interviews with famous and influential touring musicians are included.

The Ultimate Guitar Tone Handbook with DVD (with Rich Tozolli) (Alfred Music)
The Ultimate Guitar Tone Handbook is the definitive book for discovering that great guitar sound and making sure it records well. The book definitively outlines all the factors that make electric and acoustic guitars, and amplifiers and speaker cabinets sound the way they do, as well as the classic and modern recording and production techniques that capture great tone. *The Ultimate Guitar Tone Handbook* also features a series of interviews with expert players, technicians, recording engineers, producers and manufacturers that gives you an inside look into the business of guitar tone, and an accompanying DVD provides both an audio and visual reference point for achieving the classic sounds you hear on records.

The Studio Builder's Handbook with DVD (with Dennis Moody) (Alfred Music)
No matter how good your recording gear is, chances are you're not getting the best possible sound because of the deficiencies of your room. While you might think that it costs thousands of dollars and the services of an acoustic designer to improve your studio, the *Studio Builder's Handbook* will strip away the mystery of what makes a

great-sounding studio and show how you can make a huge difference in your room for as little as $150.

Audio Mixing Boot Camp: Hands-on Basic Training for Musicians (Alfred Music)
If you're creating your first mix and don't know where to begin, or your mixes aren't as good as you'd like them to be, this book is here to help. It features a series of hands-on mixing exercises designed to show you how to listen and work like a pro, and reveals the tips, tricks, and secrets to all the different facets of mixing, including instrument and vocal balance, panning, compression, EQ, reverb, delay, and making your mix as interesting as possible.

Audio Recording Basic Training: Hands-on Survival Manual for Musicians (Alfred Music)
A beginners' guide to producing great recordings. The book features a series of hands-on recording exercises designed to show you how to listen and work like a recording pro, and reveals the tips, tricks and secrets to all the different facets of recording, including miking a drum kit, recording vocals, and miking electric and acoustic instruments.

Abbey Road To Ziggy Stardust (with Ken Scott) (Alfred Music)
The memoir of legendary producer/engineer Ken Scott, who holds a unique place in music history as one of only five engineers to have recorded the Beatles and was producer and/or engineer on six David Bowie records (among his many other credits). In this funny, poignant, and honest account, Ken pulls no punches, telling it as he saw it.

BOBBY OWSINSKI LYNDA.COM VIDEO COURSES

Audio Mixing Boot Camp. Almost nine hours of movies outlining the various steps, tips, and tricks of mixing like the pros.

Audio Recording Techniques. A five-and-a-half-hour course that describes how to record crisp, rich vocals and instrument tracks and covers the process of miking and tracking a complete song using A-list session musicians in a top-of-the-line studio.

Mastering for iTunes. A short video that demonstrates best practices for mastering music and audio destined for sale on Apple iTunes with its new Mastered for iTunes high-resolution audio program.

Audio Mastering Techniques. A two-hour video that explores essential mastering concepts and techniques used by experienced audio engineers to create a cohesive album from a set of mixed tracks.

Also Available From Bobby Owsinski

Delay Genie iPhone App: Time your delays and reverbs to the track with this free, easy-to-use app that also has a live mode for delaying speakers or delay towers.

Bobby Owsinski's Social Media Connections

Bobby's Music Production Blog: bobbyowsinski.blogspot.com

Bobby's Music Industry Blog: music3point0.blogspot.com

Bobby on Facebook: facebook.com/bobby.owsinski

Bobby on YouTube: youtube.com/polymedia

Bobby on LinkedIn: linkedin.com/in/bobbyo

Bobby on Twitter: @bobbyowsinski

About Bobby Owsinski

A long-time music industry veteran, Bobby Owsinski started his career as a guitar and keyboard player, songwriter, and arranger, eventually becoming an in-demand producer/engineer working not only with a variety of recording artists, but on commercials, television, and motion pictures as well. He was one of the first to delve into surround sound music mixing, and has worked on more than 100 surround projects and DVD productions for a variety of superstar acts.

By combining his music and reording experience with an accessible writing style, Bobby has become one of the best-selling authors in the music recording industry. His 18 books are staples in audio recording, music, and music business programs in colleges around the world.

Bobby is a frequent speaker at universities and industry conferences the world over, he has served as the longtime producer of the annual Surround Music Awards, and he is one of the creators and executive producers for the Guitar Universe and *Desert Island Music* television programs.

Bobby's blogs are some of the most influential and widely read in the music business. Visit Bobby's production blog at bobbyowsinski.blogspot.com, his Music 3.0 music industry blog at music3point0.blogspot.com, his postings at Forbes at forbes.com/sites/bobbyowsinski/, and his website at bobbyowsinski.com.